# THE ESSENTIAL GUIDE TO HOSPICE CHAPLAINCY

*Comprehensive Insights, Practices, and a Professional Guide*

Dr. Maxwell Shimba

SHIMBA
PUBLISHING

# TABLE OF CONTENTS

# INTRODUCTION

The Sacred Role of a Hospice Chaplain

In the twilight moments of life, as individuals approach their final days, a unique and profound type of care becomes paramount—one that addresses not just the physical and emotional needs, but the spiritual ones as well. This is where the role of the hospice chaplain emerges as both sacred and essential. Providing spiritual care at the end of life, a hospice chaplain offers solace, comfort, and a sense of peace to patients and their families as they navigate the often daunting journey toward death.

The hospice movement itself is rooted in the philosophy of providing holistic care. Originating in the mid-20th century, it aims to affirm life and regard dying as a normal process. Hospice care neither hastens nor postpones death but focuses on providing relief from pain and other distressing symptoms. Within this framework, the spiritual dimension of care is as critical as the physical and emotional aspects.

Hospice chaplains, often unsung heroes in the healthcare system, play a pivotal role in this delicate phase of life. They stand as beacons of hope, providing a non-judgmental, compassionate presence that helps patients find meaning, reconcile with their beliefs, and achieve a sense of closure. Their work is not confined to any single faith or religious tradition. Instead, it encompasses a broad spectrum of spiritual expressions, ensuring that the diverse needs of patients are met with respect and empathy.

The sacredness of the hospice chaplain's role lies in their ability to connect deeply with individuals at their most vulnerable moments. It involves listening with the heart, offering prayers, facilitating rituals, and sometimes simply being there in silence. For many patients, the presence of a chaplain can be a source of profound comfort, helping them face their fears, express their final wishes, and make peace with their journey's end.

Family members, too, find solace in the support provided by hospice chaplains. The impending loss of a loved one brings with it a whirlwind of emotions—grief, guilt, anxiety, and often, a crisis of faith. Chaplains offer a steady hand, guiding families through their grief, helping them understand and cope with their emotions, and providing a space to express their sorrow and love. They also play a critical role in post-death bereavement, supporting families as they begin the difficult process of mourning and adjustment.

The importance of the hospice chaplain's role is increasingly recognized within the healthcare community. As the population ages and more people face chronic illnesses, the demand for compassionate, end-of-life care continues to grow. Hospice chaplains are trained to meet this demand, and equipped with the skills to address complex spiritual and existential issues that arise at the end of life.

In the chapters that follow, this book will delve into the various dimensions of hospice chaplaincy. We will explore the day-to-day experiences of chaplains, the methods they use to provide comfort, and the profound impact they have on patients and families. Through personal testimonies, case studies, and reflections, we will uncover the depth and breadth of this sacred vocation.

We will also address the challenges faced by hospice chaplains, including ethical dilemmas, emotional strain, and the need for continual professional development. The book aims to provide a comprehensive guide for current and aspiring hospice chaplains, offering insights and practical advice to support them in their vital work.

Ultimately, "Faith at Life's End: The Role of a Hospice Chaplain" is a tribute to those who dedicate their lives to walking with others through the valley of the shadow of death. It is an exploration of how spiritual care at the end of life can bring peace, meaning, and grace to those on the final leg of their earthly journey. Whether you are a healthcare professional, a family member, or simply someone interested in the profound intersection of spirituality and end-of-life care, this book offers valuable perspectives and heartfelt stories that illuminate the sacred work of hospice chaplains.

## PURPOSE AND STRUCTURE

The purpose of "Faith at Life's End: The Role of a Hospice Chaplain" is to provide a comprehensive understanding of the vital role hospice chaplains play in end-of-life care. This book aims to illuminate the profound impact that spiritual care can have on patients and their families as they navigate the complex emotions and existential questions that arise during the final stages of life. By exploring the various dimensions of hospice chaplaincy, this book seeks to inspire, educate, and provide practical guidance to current and aspiring chaplains, as well as to those involved in hospice care and interested in the intersection of spirituality and end-of-life issues.

Structure of the Book

This book is structured to guide the reader through the multifaceted role of a hospice chaplain, offering insights, personal stories, and practical advice. The chapters are organized to progressively build a comprehensive picture of hospice chaplaincy, from its foundational concepts to its day-to-day practices, challenges, and future directions.

Chapter 1: The Calling of a Hospice Chaplain

- This chapter explores the unique calling of hospice chaplains, including the qualities and motivations that draw individuals to this sacred vocation. It includes personal testimonies from chaplains about their journey into hospice care.

Chapter 2: Comforting the Dying

- Focused on the core of hospice chaplaincy, this chapter delves into the techniques and approaches used by chaplains to provide comfort and spiritual care to dying patients. Real-life case studies illustrate the profound impact of a chaplain's presence.

Chapter 3: The Journey of a Hospice Chaplain

- This chapter offers a glimpse into the daily life of a hospice chaplain, highlighting the challenges and rewards of their work. Personal reflections from experienced chaplains provide deeper insights into their journey.

Chapter 4: End-of-Life Grace

- Exploring the concept of grace at the end of life, this chapter discusses how chaplains help facilitate grace-filled moments for patients and their families. Inspirational stories showcase these transformative experiences.

Chapter 5: Shepherding Souls

- This chapter addresses the dual role of hospice chaplains in supporting both patients and their families. It examines the long-term impact of chaplaincy care and how chaplains continue to influence families after a patient's passing.

Chapter 6: Spiritual Tools and Practices

- A practical guide to the various spiritual tools and practices used by hospice chaplains, including prayer, meditation, and religious rituals. This chapter provides actionable advice for chaplains to enhance their care.

Chapter 7: Interfaith and Multicultural Approaches

- With a focus on inclusivity, this chapter discusses how chaplains provide spiritual care in a multicultural and multi-faith context. Strategies for addressing diverse spiritual needs are highlighted.

Chapter 8: Challenges and Ethical Dilemmas

- This chapter explores the common challenges and ethical dilemmas faced by hospice chaplains, such as maintaining professional boundaries and dealing with emotional strain. It offers practical solutions and coping strategies.

Chapter 9: Training and Development

- Aimed at current and aspiring chaplains, this chapter outlines the educational pathways and training required for hospice chaplaincy. The importance of continual learning and professional development is emphasized.

Chapter 10: Reflections and Future Directions

- The final chapter looks toward the future of hospice chaplaincy, discussing emerging trends and the evolving landscape of this field. Experienced chaplains share their reflections on the past and future of their vocation.

Conclusion

- The conclusion summarizes the key insights from the book and offers words of encouragement for hospice chaplains. It reiterates the importance of their role in providing spiritual care at the end of life.

Appendix

- The appendix includes resources for chaplains, such as recommended books, organizations, and training programs. Reflection questions are provided for personal or group discussion.

References

- A comprehensive list of references cited throughout the book, providing additional reading and resources for further exploration.

This structured approach ensures that readers gain a thorough understanding of the hospice chaplain's role, equipped with both theoretical knowledge and practical insights to support their important work in end-of-life care.

DR. MAXWELL SHIMBA

---

# CHAPTER 01

# THE CALLING OF A HOSPICE CHAPLAIN

Understanding the Role

The role of a hospice chaplain is deeply rooted in the ancient traditions of pastoral care, yet uniquely tailored to meet the profound needs of those approaching the end of life. As healthcare professionals, hospice chaplains provide a blend of spiritual, emotional, and psychological support, serving as beacons of hope and comfort in the midst of life's most challenging moments. Understanding the responsibilities and unique aspects of their calling is crucial to appreciating the invaluable contributions they make to hospice care.

The Responsibilities of a Hospice Chaplain

At its core, the role of a hospice chaplain is to provide spiritual care that respects the individual beliefs and needs of each patient and their family. This includes:

1. Spiritual Assessment and Support: Hospice chaplains conduct thorough spiritual assessments to understand the beliefs, values, and spiritual needs of their patients. This involves deep listening and creating a safe space for patients to express their fears, hopes, and spiritual concerns. The chaplain then develops a tailored plan of care to address these needs, offering prayers, meditations, or rituals as appropriate.

2. Emotional and Psychological Support: Beyond spiritual care, hospice chaplains offer emotional support to help patients and their families cope with the emotional turmoil that often accompanies the end of life. This can include counseling sessions, grief support, and simply being a compassionate presence during difficult times.

3. Facilitating Communication: One of the chaplain's key roles is to facilitate open and honest communication among patients, families, and healthcare providers. This helps ensure that everyone involved is on the same page regarding the patient's wishes, care plan, and any end-of-life decisions that need to be made.

4. End-of-Life Rituals and Sacraments: For many patients, participating in religious rituals or receiving sacraments is a crucial aspect of their end-of-life journey. Hospice chaplains provide or arrange for these services,

ensuring that the patient's spiritual needs are met according to their faith tradition.

5. Bereavement Support: The chaplain's role extends beyond the patient's death, providing ongoing support to the family through the bereavement process. This can include memorial services, grief counseling, and regular check-ins to offer continued care and support.

6. Interdisciplinary Collaboration: Hospice chaplains are integral members of the hospice care team, working closely with doctors, nurses, social workers, and other healthcare professionals to provide holistic care. This collaboration ensures that the patient's physical, emotional, and spiritual needs are all addressed in a coordinated and comprehensive manner.

The Unique Aspects of Their Calling

The calling of a hospice chaplain is unique in several profound ways:

1. A Ministry of Presence: One of the most distinctive aspects of a hospice chaplain's work is the ministry of presence. This involves being fully present with patients and families, offering a calm, non-judgmental, and compassionate presence that provides comfort and solace. This presence is often more powerful than words and can bring profound peace to those nearing the end of life.

2. Navigating Diverse Beliefs: Hospice chaplains must be adept at navigating a wide range of spiritual and religious beliefs. They are called to provide care that is inclusive and respectful of all faith traditions, as well as to those who may identify as spiritual but not religious. This requires a deep understanding of and sensitivity to diverse spiritual practices and philosophies.

3. Confronting Mortality: Working in hospice care means confronting mortality on a daily basis. Chaplains are called to help patients and families face the reality of death, providing a sense of peace and acceptance. This aspect of their calling requires a strong personal faith and resilience, as well as a deep commitment to their spiritual practice and self-care.

4. Creating Sacred Space: Hospice chaplains are skilled at creating sacred spaces wherever they go, whether it's in a patient's home, a hospital room, or a hospice facility. They bring an atmosphere of reverence and peace, helping to transform ordinary spaces into places of spiritual significance.

5. Witnessing Transformation: Hospice chaplains often witness profound transformations as patients and families navigate the end-of-life journey. This can include reconciliation with estranged loved ones, profound spiritual awakenings, and moments of grace and peace that defy

explanation. Being a part of these transformations is both a privilege and a testament to the power of spiritual care.

Personal Testimonies

To better understand the calling of a hospice chaplain, it is helpful to hear from those who have dedicated their lives to this sacred work. Here are a few personal testimonies from experienced hospice chaplains:

Chaplain Sarah's Story: "I felt called to hospice chaplaincy after experiencing the loss of my own grandmother. She received hospice care, and the chaplain who visited her made such a profound difference in her final days. I saw firsthand the peace and comfort that spiritual care can bring, and I knew that this was the path I was meant to follow. Every day, I feel honored to walk with patients and their families during such a sacred time."

Chaplain John's Journey: "My journey to becoming a hospice chaplain began with a career in pastoral ministry. I always felt a deep connection to those who were suffering and in need of spiritual support. When I made the transition to hospice care, I found that my skills and calling were a perfect fit. The work is challenging, but it is also incredibly rewarding. I am constantly amazed by the strength and resilience of the human spirit."

Chaplain Maria's Experience: "As a hospice chaplain, I have the privilege of witnessing the full spectrum of human emotions—grief, fear, love, and hope. Each patient and family I work with teaches me something new about life and faith. It is a humbling experience, and I am grateful for the opportunity to serve in this way. The connections I make with patients and their families are deeply meaningful and remind me of the importance of compassion and presence."

These testimonies highlight the deep sense of calling and commitment that hospice chaplains bring to their work. Their experiences underscore the importance of this role in providing holistic, compassionate care at the end of life.

The role of a hospice chaplain is both challenging and deeply rewarding. It requires a unique blend of spiritual insight, emotional resilience, and compassionate presence. By understanding the responsibilities and unique aspects of their calling, we can better appreciate the invaluable contributions hospice chaplains make to end-of-life care. As we journey through the subsequent chapters of this book, we will delve deeper into the practical, emotional, and spiritual dimensions of this sacred vocation, offering a comprehensive guide to the life and work of a hospice chaplain.

# PERSONAL TESTIMONIES

Stories of Individuals Who Felt Called to This Sacred Vocation

The calling to become a hospice chaplain is a profound and deeply personal journey. Each chaplain's story is unique, shaped by their experiences, faith, and the moments that drew them to this sacred vocation. In this chapter, we will hear from several hospice chaplains who have graciously shared their personal testimonies. Their stories offer a glimpse into the heart and soul of hospice chaplaincy, illustrating the powerful call to serve those at the end of life.

Chaplain Sarah's Story: A Grandmother's Peace

Sarah's journey to becoming a hospice chaplain began with a personal experience that transformed her life. She recalls:

"I never thought I would become a chaplain. My background was in education, and I loved teaching. But everything changed when my grandmother fell ill. She was placed in hospice care, and I saw firsthand the incredible impact the hospice team had on her final days. The chaplain who visited my grandmother brought a sense of peace and comfort that words cannot fully describe. He listened to her stories, prayed with her, and simply sat by her side when she needed companionship. Witnessing this, I felt a stirring in my heart. I realized that I wanted to bring that same sense of peace to others in their final days.

After my grandmother passed away, I couldn't shake the feeling that I was being called to something new. I enrolled in a pastoral care training program and eventually found my way to hospice chaplaincy. Every day, I feel honored to walk with patients and their families during such a sacred time. The work is challenging, but it is also incredibly rewarding. I know that this is where I am meant to be."

Sarah's story highlights the profound impact that hospice care can have on families and how personal experiences can lead to a calling in hospice chaplaincy.

Chaplain John's Journey: From Pastoral Ministry to Hospice Care

John's path to hospice chaplaincy was rooted in his career in pastoral ministry. He shares:

"I always felt a deep connection to those who were suffering and in need of spiritual support. As a pastor, I spent a lot of time visiting parishioners in hospitals and nursing homes. I found these visits to be some of the most meaningful aspects of my ministry. I realized that my true passion was in providing spiritual care to those who were nearing the end of life.

Making the transition to hospice care felt like a natural step for me. I completed additional training in palliative care and began working as a hospice chaplain. The work is challenging, and it requires a great deal of emotional resilience. But it is also incredibly rewarding. I am constantly amazed by the strength and resilience of the human spirit. Every patient I meet teaches me something new about faith, hope, and the power of human connection.

One of the most profound experiences I've had was with a patient named Mary. She was in her late 80s and had been diagnosed with terminal cancer. Mary was deeply spiritual, but she had many unresolved questions about her faith. We spent hours talking about her beliefs, her doubts, and her hopes for the afterlife. In her final days, Mary found a sense of peace and acceptance. Being able to walk with her on that journey was one of the greatest honors of my life."

John's story underscores the deep sense of fulfillment that comes from providing spiritual care to those at the end of life and the seamless transition from pastoral ministry to hospice chaplaincy.

Chaplain Maria's Experience: Witnessing Transformation

Maria's calling to hospice chaplaincy was shaped by her own spiritual journey and the desire to serve others. She reflects:

"As a child, I always felt a deep connection to the spiritual world. My family was very religious, and I grew up attending church regularly. As I got older, my faith deepened, and I felt a calling to serve others. I initially pursued a career in social work, but I always felt that something was missing. I wanted to incorporate my faith into my work more fully.

I decided to become a chaplain and began working in a hospital setting. It was there that I discovered my passion for end-of-life care. I realized that providing spiritual support to patients and their families during their final days was incredibly meaningful to me. I completed specialized training in hospice chaplaincy and began working with a hospice organization.

One of the most memorable experiences I've had was with a patient named Carlos. He was a young man in his 30s, diagnosed with a terminal illness. Carlos was struggling with anger and resentment about his situation. We spent many hours talking about his feelings, his fears, and his hopes for reconciliation with his family. Over time, Carlos experienced a profound transformation. He was able to forgive, find peace, and reconnect with his loved ones. Witnessing this transformation was incredibly powerful and reaffirmed my calling to this work.

Every day, I feel grateful for the opportunity to serve as a hospice chaplain. The connections I make with patients and their families are deeply meaningful, and they remind me of the importance of compassion and presence. This work is not just a job; it is a calling that brings profound fulfillment."

Maria's story illustrates the transformative power of hospice chaplaincy and the deep connections that chaplains form with their patients and families.

The personal testimonies of Chaplains Sarah, John, and Maria offer a glimpse into the heart of hospice chaplaincy. Each of their stories is a testament to the profound calling that draws individuals to this sacred vocation. Through their experiences, we see the importance of providing spiritual care at the end of life and the incredible impact it can have on patients and their families.

As we continue to explore the role of the hospice chaplain in the subsequent chapters, these personal testimonies will serve as a foundation for understanding the depth and breadth of this sacred work. The calling of a hospice chaplain is one of compassion, presence, and unwavering support, providing a beacon of hope and comfort during life's most challenging moments.

CHAPTER 02

---

# COMFORTING THE DYING

Spiritual Care Techniques

The role of a hospice chaplain is multifaceted, encompassing various methods and approaches to provide comfort and spiritual care to those nearing the end of life. This chapter explores the diverse techniques that chaplains use to address the spiritual, emotional, and psychological needs of patients and their families. Through these methods, chaplains offer solace, facilitate healing, and help patients find peace in their final days.

Listening with the Heart

One of the most fundamental techniques in providing spiritual care is active listening. This involves more than just hearing words; it requires the chaplain to be fully present, offering undivided attention and empathy.

- Active Listening: Chaplains listen attentively to patients' stories, fears, and concerns. They acknowledge the patient's feelings and provide a safe space for them to express their emotions without judgment. This form of listening helps patients feel understood and valued.

- Reflective Listening: Reflecting back what the patient has said can help clarify their thoughts and feelings. This technique involves paraphrasing the patient's words and asking open-ended questions to encourage deeper reflection and conversation.

Prayer and Meditation

Prayer and meditation are powerful tools in spiritual care, offering comfort, peace, and a sense of connection to a higher power.

- Personalized Prayers: Chaplains often create personalized prayers that resonate with the patient's beliefs and experiences. These prayers can be spoken aloud, written, or even sung, depending on the patient's preferences.

- Guided Meditation: Meditation techniques, such as guided imagery or breathing exercises, can help patients relax and find inner peace. Chaplains lead patients through these practices, helping them focus on positive images or thoughts that bring comfort.

- Rituals and Sacraments: Many patients find solace in religious rituals and sacraments. Chaplains facilitate these practices, such as administering communion, anointing with oil, or leading a final blessing, according to the patient's faith tradition.

Life Review and Storytelling

Reflecting on one's life and sharing stories can be a therapeutic and meaningful process for patients nearing the end of life.

- Life Review: Chaplains guide patients through a life review, encouraging them to reflect on their experiences, achievements, and relationships. This process can help patients find meaning, resolve unfinished business, and achieve a sense of closure.

- Storytelling: Sharing stories allows patients to express their identity and legacy. Chaplains listen to these stories, often recording or writing them down for the patient and their family to cherish. This practice can be particularly healing for both the patient and their loved ones.

Emotional and Psychological Support

Providing emotional and psychological support is a critical aspect of hospice chaplaincy, helping patients and families cope with the emotional challenges of end-of-life care.

- Grief Counseling: Chaplains offer counseling to patients and families, helping them navigate the complex emotions associated with impending loss. This includes providing tools and strategies for managing grief, fear, and anxiety.

- Presence and Companionship: Sometimes, the most powerful form of support is simply being present. Chaplains offer companionship, sitting with patients in silence, holding their hands, or sharing moments of reflection. This presence provides a sense of comfort and security.

- Validation of Emotions: Chaplains validate the emotions of patients and families, acknowledging their pain, anger, or sadness. By normalizing these feelings, chaplains help individuals feel less isolated and more understood.

Facilitating Communication

Effective communication is essential in hospice care, ensuring that patients' wishes are understood and respected.

- Family Meetings: Chaplains often facilitate family meetings to discuss the patient's wishes, care plans, and any unresolved issues. These meetings provide a space for open and honest communication, helping families come together in support of the patient.

- Advance Care Planning: Chaplains assist patients in advance care planning, helping them articulate their preferences for end-of-life care. This includes discussing living wills, healthcare proxies, and other directives that ensure the patient's wishes are honored.

Creating Sacred Space

Transforming ordinary spaces into sacred environments can provide a sense of peace and reverence for patients and their families.

- Personalized Sacred Spaces: Chaplains help create personalized sacred spaces in the patient's room, using items such as candles, religious symbols, or cherished objects. These spaces serve as a focal point for prayer, meditation, and reflection.

- Rituals of Transition: Chaplains lead rituals of transition, marking significant moments such as the end of treatment, the onset of hospice care, or the final days of life. These rituals provide structure and meaning, helping patients and families navigate these transitions with grace.

Incorporating Interfaith Approaches

Hospice chaplains must be adept at providing spiritual care that respects and honors diverse beliefs and traditions.

- Cultural Competence: Chaplains educate themselves about the cultural and religious backgrounds of their patients, ensuring that their care is respectful and inclusive. This includes understanding different religious practices, dietary restrictions, and end-of-life rituals.

- Interfaith Dialogue: Engaging in interfaith dialogue allows chaplains to connect with patients from various faith traditions. By acknowledging and celebrating these differences, chaplains build trust and create a more inclusive environment.

Case Studies

To illustrate these spiritual care techniques in practice, consider the following case studies:

Case Study 1: Finding Peace through Life Review

Mrs. Johnson, an 82-year-old woman with terminal cancer, was struggling with feelings of regret and unfinished business. Chaplain Emily guided her through a life review, encouraging her to reflect on her achievements, relationships, and cherished memories. Through this process, Mrs. Johnson was able to find peace, resolve her regrets, and leave a legacy of love and wisdom for her family.

Case Study 2: Creating a Sacred Space

Mr. Ahmed, a devout Muslim, was in his final days of life. Chaplain David worked with Mr. Ahmed and his family to create a sacred space in his hospice room. They set up a prayer rug, placed a copy of the Quran, and arranged flowers to honor his faith. This sacred space provided Mr. Ahmed with comfort and a sense of connection to his beliefs as he approached the end of life.

Case Study 3: Facilitating Family Communication

Mrs. Lee, a 70-year-old woman with advanced heart disease, had unresolved conflicts with her children. Chaplain Maria facilitated a family meeting, creating a safe space for open and honest communication. Through guided discussions, the family was able to express their emotions, forgive past grievances, and come together in support of Mrs. Lee. This reconciliation brought peace to Mrs. Lee and her family during her final days.

Providing spiritual care to those nearing the end of life requires a diverse set of techniques and approaches. By listening with the heart, offering prayer and meditation, facilitating life reviews and storytelling, providing emotional support, creating sacred spaces, and respecting diverse beliefs, hospice chaplains offer comprehensive and compassionate care. These methods help patients find peace, meaning, and comfort as they navigate their final journey, and they support families in their time of need. As we continue to explore the role of the hospice chaplain in the following chapters, these spiritual care techniques will serve as a foundation for understanding the depth and breadth of this sacred vocation.

# CASE STUDIES

Real-Life Examples Illustrating the Impact of a Chaplain's Presence

The profound impact of a hospice chaplain's presence cannot be fully appreciated without hearing the stories of those who have experienced it firsthand. This chapter presents several real-life case studies that illustrate the significant difference a chaplain can make in the lives of patients and their families as they navigate the end-of-life journey. These stories highlight the various ways chaplains provide comfort, support, and spiritual care.

Case Study 1: Mrs. Johnson – Finding Peace through Life Review

Mrs. Evelyn Johnson, an 82-year-old woman, was admitted to hospice care with terminal cancer. She struggled with feelings of regret and unresolved issues from her past, which caused her great distress.

The Chaplain's Intervention:

Chaplain Emily was assigned to Mrs. Johnson and immediately sensed her need for emotional and spiritual reconciliation. Emily introduced the concept of a life review, a therapeutic process where patients reflect on their life experiences, achievements, and relationships.

Process:

Chaplain Emily spent several sessions with Mrs. Johnson, gently guiding her through significant moments of her life. They discussed her childhood, marriage, career, and the joys and challenges she faced. Emily encouraged Mrs. Johnson to share her stories, which she documented in a journal for Mrs. Johnson's family.

Outcome:

Through this process, Mrs. Johnson found a sense of closure and peace. She was able to express her regrets, celebrate her achievements, and feel validated in her experiences. The journal became a treasured keepsake for her family, preserving her legacy and providing comfort after her passing.

Impact:

Chaplain Emily's presence and the life review process helped Mrs. Johnson transition from distress to tranquility. This case illustrates how a chaplain can facilitate emotional healing and leave a lasting impact on both the patient and their loved ones.

Case Study 2: Mr. Ahmed – Creating a Sacred Space

Mr. Ahmed, a 65-year-old man with advanced lung disease, was deeply connected to his Muslim faith. As his condition worsened, he felt a growing need to connect with his spiritual beliefs and practices.

The Chaplain's Intervention:

Chaplain David, who had experience with interfaith spiritual care, was called to support Mr. Ahmed. Recognizing the importance of faith in Mr. Ahmed's life, David set out to create a sacred space in his hospice room.

Process:

David consulted with Mr. Ahmed and his family to understand the religious items and practices that were important to them. They brought in a prayer rug, a copy of the Quran, and arranged for the call to prayer to be played softly in the room. David also coordinated with local Muslim leaders to ensure Mr. Ahmed could receive appropriate spiritual support.

Outcome:

The transformation of Mr. Ahmed's room into a sacred space provided him with immense comfort. He was able to perform his prayers, read the Quran, and feel connected to his faith during his final days. This spiritual connection brought him peace and solace.

Impact:

David's sensitivity and proactive approach in creating a sacred space highlighted the chaplain's role in respecting and facilitating diverse spiritual practices. Mr. Ahmed's family expressed deep gratitude for the comfort and dignity this brought to his end-of-life experience.

Case Study 3: Mrs. Lee – Facilitating Family Communication

Mrs. Susan Lee, a 70-year-old woman with advanced heart disease, faced not only her illness but also unresolved conflicts within her family. These tensions were causing her significant emotional distress.

The Chaplain's Intervention:

Chaplain Maria was assigned to Mrs. Lee's case. She recognized the importance of addressing the family dynamics to bring peace to Mrs. Lee in her final days.

Process:

Maria arranged a family meeting, inviting Mrs. Lee's children and other close relatives. She facilitated the discussion, encouraging each family member to express their feelings and concerns in a respectful and open manner. Maria used reflective listening and mediation techniques to guide the conversation toward reconciliation.

Outcome:

The family meeting allowed Mrs. Lee and her children to address long-standing issues and misunderstandings. Through the conversation, they expressed forgiveness, shared their love, and came together in support of Mrs. Lee.

Impact:

Maria's facilitation helped transform a tense and painful situation into a moment of healing and connection. Mrs. Lee's final days were filled with the love and support of her reconciled family, providing her with deep emotional comfort.

Case Study 4: Mr. Thompson – Emotional and Psychological Support

Mr. Robert Thompson, a 78-year-old man with end-stage renal disease, was experiencing severe anxiety and fear about dying. His condition left him feeling isolated and hopeless.

The Chaplain's Intervention:

Chaplain James, known for his compassionate presence, was assigned to Mr. Thompson. Understanding the importance of addressing emotional and psychological distress, James focused on providing consistent support and companionship.

Process:

James visited Mr. Thompson regularly, offering a listening ear and a comforting presence. He engaged Mr. Thompson in conversations about his fears and anxieties, validating his feelings and providing reassurance. James also introduced relaxation techniques such as deep breathing exercises and guided imagery to help Mr. Thompson manage his anxiety.

Outcome:

Over time, Mr. Thompson began to open up about his fears and found solace in James' presence. The relaxation techniques helped reduce his anxiety, and the consistent support provided by James helped Mr. Thompson feel less isolated and more at peace.

Impact:

James' dedication to providing emotional and psychological support significantly improved Mr. Thompson's quality of life. This case demonstrates the vital role chaplains play in addressing the holistic needs of patients.

Case Study 5: Mrs. Garcia – Prayer and Meditation

Mrs. Maria Garcia, a 60-year-old woman with metastatic breast cancer, found great comfort in her Catholic faith. As she neared the end of her life, she expressed a strong desire for spiritual support through prayer and meditation.

The Chaplain's Intervention:

Chaplain Teresa, who had a deep understanding of Catholic traditions, was assigned to Mrs. Garcia. Teresa recognized the importance of incorporating Mrs. Garcia's faith into her end-of-life care.

Process:

Teresa spent time with Mrs. Garcia, praying the Rosary together and reading passages from the Bible. She also led guided meditations that focused on comforting scriptures and images of peace. Teresa arranged for a priest to visit and administer the sacraments of the Anointing of the Sick and Holy Communion.

Outcome:

The regular prayers, meditations, and sacraments provided Mrs. Garcia with immense spiritual comfort and a sense of closeness to her faith. These practices helped her feel connected to God and brought her peace in her final days.

Impact:

Teresa's integration of prayer and meditation into Mrs. Garcia's care highlights the importance of spiritual practices in providing end-of-life comfort. The spiritual support significantly eased Mrs. Garcia's journey, reinforcing the chaplain's role in facilitating faith-based care.

These case studies illustrate the profound impact that hospice chaplains can have on the lives of patients and their families. Through active listening, prayer, meditation, life review, emotional support, creating sacred spaces, and facilitating communication, chaplains provide holistic care that addresses the spiritual, emotional, and psychological needs of those nearing the end of life. The presence and support of a chaplain can transform the end-of-life experience, bringing peace, comfort, and meaning to patients and their loved ones. As we continue to explore the role of hospice chaplains in the following chapters, these real-life examples serve as powerful testimonies to the essential and sacred work they perform.

---

# CHAPTER 03

## THE JOURNEY OF A HOSPICE CHAPLAIN

Day-to-Day Experiences: A Typical Day in the Life of a Hospice Chaplain

The life of a hospice chaplain is a tapestry woven with moments of profound connection, spiritual support, and emotional resilience. Each day presents new challenges and rewards, as chaplains navigate the delicate balance of providing care to those at the end of life. This chapter explores a typical day in the life of a hospice chaplain, highlighting the unique experiences, obstacles, and fulfillment that come with this sacred vocation.

Morning Routine: Preparing for the Day

A hospice chaplain's day often begins early, with a routine that includes personal reflection and preparation for the day ahead. Many chaplains start their mornings with meditation, prayer, or a quiet moment to center themselves and seek strength for the tasks that lie ahead. This time of spiritual grounding is essential, as it allows chaplains to approach their work with a clear mind and an open heart.

Example: Chaplain Sarah

Chaplain Sarah begins her day with a cup of tea and a few minutes of silent meditation. She reviews her schedule, noting the patients she will visit and any special needs or requests they have. She also takes a moment to read a passage from a favorite inspirational book, which helps her feel connected to her own spirituality and ready to offer support to others.

Morning Visits: Providing Spiritual Care

The core of a chaplain's workday involves visiting patients, either in their homes, hospice facilities, or hospitals. Each visit is unique, tailored to the specific needs and desires of the patient and their family.

Example: Chaplain James

Chaplain James's first visit of the day is to see Mr. Thompson, a patient who has been struggling with severe anxiety. James spends time listening to Mr. Thompson's concerns, offering words of comfort and reassurance. He leads Mr. Thompson in a guided meditation, helping him find a moment of peace amidst his fears. Before leaving, James offers a prayer, tailored to Mr. Thompson's faith tradition, which brings a visible sense of calm to the patient.

Interdisciplinary Team Meetings: Collaborative Care

Hospice chaplains are integral members of the interdisciplinary care team, which includes doctors, nurses, social workers, and other healthcare professionals. These team meetings are crucial for discussing patient care plans, sharing insights, and ensuring that all aspects of a patient's needs are being addressed.

Example: Chaplain Maria

Chaplain Maria joins the interdisciplinary team meeting at the hospice facility where she works. The team discusses the current status of each patient, including their physical, emotional, and spiritual needs. Maria shares her observations and offers suggestions for additional spiritual support for certain patients. Her input is valued, as it provides a holistic perspective on patient care.

Afternoon Visits: Deepening Connections

Afternoons are often reserved for longer visits with patients and their families. These visits can include more in-depth conversations, life reviews, or participation in rituals and sacraments.

Example: Chaplain David

Chaplain David spends the afternoon with Mrs. Garcia, a devout Catholic patient. He brings a Rosary and together they pray, reflecting on the mysteries and seeking comfort in their faith. David listens as Mrs. Garcia shares her life story, capturing her memories and experiences in a journal that will be given to her family. This time together not only provides spiritual solace for Mrs. Garcia but also strengthens her connection to her faith and her legacy.

Providing Emotional Support: Listening and Presence

One of the most critical aspects of a chaplain's role is providing emotional support through active listening and compassionate presence. This involves being fully present with patients and their families, offering a safe space for them to express their fears, hopes, and emotions.

Example: Chaplain Emily

Chaplain Emily visits Mr. Ahmed, who is in the final stages of his illness. Mr. Ahmed is experiencing a range of emotions, from fear to acceptance. Emily sits with him, holding his hand and listening as he talks about his life and his feelings about death. She validates his emotions, assuring him that it's okay to feel a mixture of sadness and peace. Her presence provides immense comfort to Mr. Ahmed, who feels heard and understood.

Addressing Challenges: Emotional Resilience and Self-Care

The work of a hospice chaplain is emotionally demanding, and it's essential for chaplains to practice self-care and seek support when needed. This can include regular supervision, peer support groups, or personal therapeutic practices.

Example: Chaplain John

Chaplain John experiences a particularly challenging day, with multiple visits to patients who are in significant distress. He takes time at the end of the day to debrief with a colleague, sharing his experiences and emotions. This peer support helps John process the day's events and reinforces the importance of taking care of his own emotional well-being.

Evening Reflections: Finding Meaning in the Day

As the day draws to a close, many chaplains take time to reflect on their experiences, find meaning in their interactions, and prepare for the days ahead. This reflection can be a deeply spiritual practice, helping chaplains stay connected to their calling and their sense of purpose.

Example: Chaplain Teresa

Chaplain Teresa ends her day with a journal entry, capturing the moments that stood out to her and the emotions she felt. She writes about the patients she visited, the conversations that touched her heart, and the prayers that brought comfort. This practice helps Teresa process her day, find closure, and renew her commitment to her work.

Conclusion: The Rewards of Hospice Chaplaincy

The journey of a hospice chaplain is marked by profound challenges and deep rewards. Each day, chaplains offer spiritual care, emotional support, and compassionate presence to those facing the end of life. The impact of their work is immeasurable, providing comfort, peace, and a sense of meaning to patients and their families.

The daily experiences of a hospice chaplain highlight the resilience, dedication, and spiritual depth required for this sacred vocation. Through their presence and support, chaplains bring light to some of life's darkest moments, helping individuals and families navigate the end-of-life journey with grace and dignity. As we continue to explore the role of hospice chaplains in the following chapters, these day-to-day experiences serve as a testament to the vital and transformative nature of their work.

## REFLECTIONS AND INSIGHTS

Reflections and Insights: Personal Reflections from Experienced Chaplains on Their Journey

The journey of a hospice chaplain is deeply personal, filled with moments of profound connection, spiritual growth, and emotional challenges. This chapter shares the reflections and insights of experienced hospice chaplains, offering a glimpse into their inner worlds and the wisdom they have gained through their sacred work. Their stories highlight the transformative power of hospice chaplaincy and the enduring impact it has on both the chaplains and the individuals they serve.

Chaplain Sarah: Finding Meaning in Presence

Reflection:

"My journey as a hospice chaplain has taught me the incredible value of presence. When I first started, I felt pressure to say the right things and provide answers to unanswerable questions. Over time, I realized that my presence was often enough. Just being there, holding a patient's hand, or sitting quietly with a grieving family can bring immense comfort. It's a humbling experience to witness the peace that can come from simply being present with someone in their most vulnerable moments."

Insight:

"The most profound connections often happen in silence. In those quiet moments, a deep spiritual exchange occurs that transcends words. I've learned to embrace these moments and trust that my presence is a gift in itself."

Chaplain James: The Power of Listening

Reflection:

"One of the most important lessons I've learned is the power of listening. Patients and families often have so much they need to express, and simply listening can be incredibly healing. I remember a patient named Alice who was struggling with feelings of guilt and regret. She needed someone to listen without judgment. Through our conversations, she was able to find forgiveness and peace. Listening is a sacred act that can facilitate profound healing."

Insight:

"Active listening requires full attention and an open heart. It's about being fully present and creating a safe space for others to share their deepest thoughts and emotions. This simple act can transform a person's end-of-life experience."

Chaplain Maria: Embracing Diverse Beliefs

Reflection:

"Hospice chaplaincy has exposed me to a rich tapestry of beliefs and spiritual practices. I've worked with patients from various faith traditions and those who identify as spiritual but not religious. Each encounter has deepened my understanding and respect for different paths to the divine. I recall working with a Buddhist patient who taught me the beauty of mindful presence and acceptance. These experiences have enriched my own spiritual journey and expanded my worldview."

Insight:

"Every patient brings a unique spiritual perspective, and it's essential to honor and respect that. Embracing diverse beliefs not only enhances our ability to provide meaningful care but also broadens our own spiritual horizons."

Chaplain David: The Gift of Transformation

Reflection:

"I've witnessed remarkable transformations in patients and families. One of the most memorable was a man named John who had been estranged from his daughter for years. As he approached the end of his life, he expressed a deep desire for reconciliation. With gentle guidance and support, he was able to reconnect with his daughter, and they shared a heartfelt reunion. These moments of transformation remind me of the profound impact we can have as chaplains."

Insight:

"End-of-life can be a time of healing and reconciliation. Our role is to facilitate these opportunities for transformation, helping patients and families find peace and closure. It's a powerful reminder of the resilience and strength of the human spirit."

Chaplain Emily: Navigating Emotional Challenges

Reflection:

"The emotional challenges of hospice chaplaincy are significant, but they are also what make this work so meaningful. There are days when the grief and sadness feel overwhelming, but I've learned the importance of self-care and seeking support. Connecting with fellow chaplains and engaging in regular spiritual practices helps me stay grounded. Despite the emotional weight, the privilege of being with people in their final moments far outweighs the challenges."

Insight:

"Self-care is essential for sustaining this work. By taking care of ourselves, we can continue to offer compassionate and effective support to our patients and their families. It's a reminder that we, too, are human and need nurturing."

Chaplain John: The Role of Faith

Reflection:

"My faith is the foundation of my work as a hospice chaplain. It gives me strength, guidance, and a sense of purpose. I've seen how faith can provide immense comfort and hope to patients facing the end of life. For some, it's a source of peace; for others, it brings up questions and doubts. Regardless of where they are on their spiritual journey, my faith helps me provide the support they need. It's a privilege to walk alongside them and share in their spiritual journey."

Insight:

"Faith can be a powerful source of comfort and resilience. Our role as chaplains is to support patients in their faith journey, helping them find meaning and peace as they approach the end of life. It's a sacred responsibility that requires deep empathy and compassion."

Conclusion: The Heart of Hospice Chaplaincy

The reflections and insights shared by these experienced chaplains highlight the essence of hospice chaplaincy. Their journeys are marked by profound connections, emotional resilience, and deep spiritual growth. Through their stories, we see the transformative power of presence, listening, and embracing diverse beliefs. We also recognize the importance of self-care and the central role of faith in sustaining this sacred work.

As we continue to explore the role of hospice chaplains in the following chapters, these personal reflections serve as a testament to the profound impact chaplains have on the lives of those they serve. Their experiences remind us of the beauty and depth of hospice chaplaincy, a vocation that brings light and comfort to life's most challenging moments.

# CHAPTER 04

## END-OF-LIFE GRACE

Grace in Final Moments: The Concept of Grace at the End of Life and How Chaplains Facilitate This Experience

Grace, a concept that transcends religious boundaries, represents a state of dignity, peace, and profound spiritual presence. In the context of end-of-life care, grace becomes a guiding principle for hospice chaplains, who strive to help patients and their families experience a sense of peace and completeness in their final moments. This chapter delves into the concept of grace at the end of life and explores how chaplains facilitate this sacred experience.

Understanding Grace at the End of Life

Grace, in its most profound sense, can be described as an unmerited favor or a divine influence that brings a sense of peace and spiritual fulfillment. At the end of life, grace manifests as an acceptance of one's journey, a reconciliation with the past, and a peaceful transition from life to death. It is a state where patients feel enveloped by love, compassion, and a sense of completion.

The Elements of End-of-Life Grace:

- Acceptance: Coming to terms with the inevitability of death and finding peace with it.

- Reconciliation: Healing past wounds and mending broken relationships.

- Spiritual Fulfillment: Feeling connected to a higher power or finding deep inner peace.

- Dignity: Maintaining a sense of personal dignity and respect in the final moments.

- Peace: Experiencing a profound sense of calm and tranquility.

Facilitating Grace: The Role of Hospice Chaplains

Hospice chaplains play a crucial role in facilitating the experience of grace at the end of life. Through their compassionate presence, spiritual guidance, and emotional support, chaplains help patients and families navigate the final stages of life with dignity and peace.

Creating a Sacred Space:

One of the primary ways chaplains facilitate grace is by creating a sacred space for patients and their families. This involves transforming the physical environment into a place of peace and reverence.

Example: Chaplain Emily

Chaplain Emily was assigned to care for Mr. Thompson, who was in the final stages of liver cancer. Understanding the importance of a comforting environment, Emily helped Mr. Thompson's family arrange his room with his favorite flowers, soft lighting, and calming music. This sacred space provided a serene setting for Mr. Thompson's final days, helping him feel at peace and surrounded by love.

Providing Emotional and Spiritual Support:

Chaplains offer continuous emotional and spiritual support to patients and their families, helping them process their emotions and find meaning in their journey.

Example: Chaplain James

Chaplain James supported Mrs. Lee, who struggled with anxiety and fear as she faced the end of her life. Through regular visits, James listened to her fears, offered words of comfort, and prayed with her. He also introduced guided meditations that helped Mrs. Lee find moments of peace and calm. His presence and support enabled Mrs. Lee to embrace her final moments with grace and tranquility.

Facilitating Reconciliation:

Reconciliation is a critical aspect of experiencing grace at the end of life. Chaplains often help patients mend broken relationships and find forgiveness.

Example: Chaplain Maria

Chaplain Maria worked with Mr. Ahmed, who had been estranged from his son for many years. Understanding the importance of reconciliation, Maria gently encouraged Mr. Ahmed to reach out to his son. She facilitated a conversation between them, providing a safe space for both to express their feelings. This act of reconciliation brought immense peace to Mr. Ahmed, allowing him to experience grace in his final moments.

Conducting Rituals and Sacraments:

Religious rituals and sacraments can provide profound comfort and a sense of spiritual fulfillment for patients nearing the end of life.

Example: Chaplain David

Chaplain David was called to support Mrs. Garcia, a devout Catholic. He facilitated the sacraments of the Anointing of the Sick and Holy Communion, which were deeply meaningful to her. These rituals provided Mrs. Garcia with a sense of spiritual grace and connection to her faith, helping her feel at peace as she approached the end of her life.

Offering Final Blessings and Prayers:

Final blessings and prayers can be a powerful source of comfort and peace for patients and their families.

Example: Chaplain Sarah

Chaplain Sarah was present during the final moments of Mr. Johnson's life. As his family gathered around, Sarah offered a final blessing, praying for peace and comfort. This blessing provided a sense of closure and grace for both Mr. Johnson and his family, helping them feel supported and loved in their time of grief.

Stories of End-of-Life Grace

To illustrate the concept of grace at the end of life, consider the following stories of patients who experienced profound peace and fulfillment in their final moments.

Story 1: Grace through Reconciliation

Mrs. Thompson had been estranged from her sister for decades due to a family dispute. As she neared the end of her life, she expressed a deep desire to reconcile. Chaplain Emily facilitated a meeting between Mrs. Thompson and her sister, where they were able to express their feelings, forgive each other, and find peace. This reconciliation brought a profound sense of grace to Mrs. Thompson, allowing her to pass away with a healed heart.

Story 2: Spiritual Fulfillment

Mr. Ahmed, a Muslim patient, found great comfort in his faith as he approached the end of his life. Chaplain James helped create a sacred space with items important to Mr. Ahmed's faith, such as a prayer rug and the Quran. James also coordinated with local Muslim leaders to ensure Mr. Ahmed could receive appropriate spiritual support. This connection to his faith provided Mr. Ahmed with spiritual fulfillment and a sense of grace in his final days.

Story 3: Peace through Rituals

Mrs. Garcia, a Catholic patient, received immense comfort from the sacraments of her faith. Chaplain David facilitated the Anointing of the Sick and Holy Communion, which were deeply meaningful to her. These rituals provided Mrs. Garcia with a sense of spiritual grace and connection to her faith, helping her feel at peace as she approached the end of her life.

Conclusion: The Essence of End-of-Life Grace

Grace at the end of life is a multifaceted experience that encompasses acceptance, reconciliation, spiritual fulfillment, dignity, and peace. Hospice chaplains play a vital role in facilitating this experience, providing compassionate presence, emotional support, and spiritual guidance. Through their efforts, chaplains help patients and their families navigate the final stages of life with a sense of grace and tranquility.

The stories and examples shared in this chapter illustrate the profound impact chaplains can have in helping individuals experience grace in their final moments. As we continue to explore the role of hospice chaplains in the following chapters, the concept of end-of-life grace serves as a cornerstone of their sacred work, bringing light and comfort to those at the end of life.

## INSPIRATIONAL STORIES

Accounts of Grace-Filled Moments Witnessed by Chaplains

Grace at the end of life often manifests in powerful and transformative ways. Hospice chaplains witness many grace-filled moments, where profound peace, reconciliation, and spiritual fulfillment become evident. This chapter shares several inspirational stories of such moments, highlighting the incredible impact that grace can have on patients and their families during the final stages of life.

Story 1: A Daughter's Farewell

Patient: Mrs. Evelyn Johnson

Chaplain: Sarah

Mrs. Evelyn Johnson was an 82-year-old woman with terminal cancer. Her daughter, Lisa, lived far away and had a difficult relationship with her mother due to past misunderstandings and unresolved issues. As Mrs. Johnson's condition worsened, she expressed a longing to see Lisa and mend their relationship before she passed away.

The Chaplain's Intervention:

Chaplain Sarah reached out to Lisa, gently encouraging her to visit her mother. After some hesitation, Lisa agreed. Chaplain Sarah facilitated their reunion, creating a calm and welcoming environment.

The Grace-Filled Moment:

When Lisa arrived, there was initial tension, but with Sarah's gentle guidance, the barriers began to break down. Mrs. Johnson expressed her regrets and love, while Lisa shared her own feelings of pain and longing for reconciliation. They embraced, shedding tears of forgiveness and love. Mrs. Johnson passed away peacefully a few days later, having reconciled with her daughter, bringing immense peace to both.

Impact:

This moment of reconciliation brought a profound sense of grace to Mrs. Johnson's final days. It also provided Lisa with the peace of knowing she had made amends with her mother, a gift that would bring her comfort for the rest of her life.

Story 2: The Music of Peace

Patient: Mr. Robert Thompson

Chaplain: James

Mr. Robert Thompson, a 78-year-old man with end-stage renal disease, loved music. As he neared the end of his life, he struggled with anxiety and fear, often finding it difficult to relax and find peace.

The Chaplain's Intervention:

Chaplain James, aware of Mr. Thompson's love for music, decided to incorporate it into his care. He brought a portable speaker and played Mr. Thompson's favorite classical pieces during their visits. James also arranged for a local musician to visit and play live music at Mr. Thompson's bedside.

The Grace-Filled Moment:

One afternoon, the musician played a particularly beautiful piece that had always been Mr. Thompson's favorite. As the music filled the room, Mr. Thompson's anxiety seemed to melt away. He closed his eyes, a serene smile spreading across his face. In that moment, surrounded by the music he loved, Mr. Thompson found a deep sense of peace and grace.

Impact:

The use of music as a therapeutic tool brought profound comfort to Mr. Thompson. It helped him find a sense of tranquility and grace, transforming his final days into a time of peace and fulfillment.

Story 3: A Father's Blessing

Patient: Mr. Ahmed

Chaplain: Maria

Mr. Ahmed, a 65-year-old man with advanced lung disease, had been estranged from his son, Ali, for several years. As he approached the end of his life, Mr. Ahmed expressed a deep desire to reconcile with Ali and give him his blessing.

The Chaplain's Intervention:

Chaplain Maria reached out to Ali, explaining his father's wishes. Ali was initially resistant, harboring feelings of anger and hurt. With patience and understanding, Maria facilitated a dialogue between father and son.

The Grace-Filled Moment:

After several conversations, Ali agreed to visit his father. When he arrived, there was a palpable tension in the room. Maria guided the conversation, helping both men express their feelings. Mr. Ahmed tearfully asked for forgiveness and offered his blessing to Ali. Moved by his father's sincerity, Ali forgave him, and they embraced, both weeping.

Impact:

This moment of reconciliation and blessing brought a profound sense of grace to Mr. Ahmed's final days. It also provided Ali with the peace of knowing he had reconnected with his father before his passing, a moment that would carry significant emotional weight for him.

Story 4: The Comfort of Faith

Patient: Mrs. Maria Garcia

Chaplain: David

Mrs. Maria Garcia, a devout Catholic, found immense comfort in her faith. As she neared the end of her life, she expressed a desire to receive the sacraments and participate in her religious rituals.

The Chaplain's Intervention:

Chaplain David arranged for a priest to visit Mrs. Garcia to administer the sacraments of Anointing of the Sick and Holy Communion. David also visited Mrs. Garcia regularly, praying the Rosary with her and reading passages from the Bible.

The Grace-Filled Moment:

During one of the visits, as Mrs. Garcia received Holy Communion, she closed her eyes and a look of profound peace came over her face. She expressed feeling deeply connected to her faith and at peace with her impending death. The sacraments and prayers brought her immense spiritual comfort and a sense of divine grace.

Impact:

The spiritual care provided by Chaplain David and the administration of the sacraments helped Mrs. Garcia experience a profound sense of grace. Her faith provided a source of strength and peace, allowing her to approach the end of her life with dignity and tranquility.

Story 5: The Circle of Love

Patient: Mr. John Thompson

Chaplain: Sarah

Mr. John Thompson, a 70-year-old man with terminal heart disease, had a large and loving family. As his condition worsened, his family struggled with the impending loss, experiencing a mix of grief and anxiety.

The Chaplain's Intervention:

Chaplain Sarah suggested a family gathering where everyone could share their feelings and support each other. She facilitated this meeting, creating a space for open communication and emotional expression.

The Grace-Filled Moment:

During the gathering, each family member shared memories, expressed their love for Mr. Thompson, and voiced their feelings about his approaching death. Mr. Thompson listened, tears streaming down his face, and then expressed his gratitude for his family's love and support. The family formed a circle around his bed, holding hands and praying together.

Impact:

This gathering brought a sense of unity and grace to Mr. Thompson's final days. It allowed the family to support each other and find peace in their shared love. Mr. Thompson's passing was surrounded by the warmth and grace of his family's love, providing him with deep emotional comfort.

These inspirational stories illustrate the profound impact of grace at the end of life. Hospice chaplains, through their compassionate presence and spiritual guidance, facilitate moments of peace, reconciliation, and spiritual fulfillment. These grace-filled moments not only bring comfort to patients but also provide lasting peace to their families.

The accounts shared in this chapter highlight the transformative power of grace and the essential role chaplains play in helping individuals and families navigate the final stages of life with dignity and peace. As we continue to explore the role of hospice chaplains in the following chapters, these stories of grace serve as a testament to the sacred and profound nature of their work.

52

---

# CHAPTER 05

## SHEPHERDING SOULS

Guiding Families and Patients: The Dual Role of Supporting Both the Patient and Their Families

Hospice chaplains hold a unique and dual responsibility in their role of shepherding souls. They are tasked with providing spiritual and emotional support not only to the patients but also to their families. This chapter explores how chaplains navigate the complexities of supporting both groups, the strategies they employ, and the profound impact of their work.

Understanding the Dual Role

The end-of-life journey is not an isolated experience for the patient alone; it profoundly affects their loved ones. Families often grapple with a range of emotions, from grief and fear to confusion and guilt. Hospice chaplains recognize that their role extends beyond the patient's bedside to the broader circle of family members, offering guidance, support, and a compassionate presence.

Key Elements of the Dual Role:

- Emotional Support: Addressing the emotional needs of both patients and families.

- Spiritual Guidance: Providing spiritual care that respects the diverse beliefs of patients and their families.

- Communication Facilitation: Ensuring clear and compassionate communication among patients, families, and healthcare teams.

- Grief Support: Helping families cope with anticipatory grief and bereavement.

Supporting Patients

Supporting patients at the end of life involves addressing their physical, emotional, and spiritual needs. Chaplains provide a listening ear, offer prayers or rituals, and help patients find peace and meaning in their final days.

Example: Chaplain Emily and Mr. Johnson

Mr. Johnson, a 75-year-old patient with terminal cancer, was deeply troubled by his impending death. He expressed fears about the afterlife and concerns about leaving his family behind. Chaplain Emily visited him regularly, listening to his fears and providing reassurance. She shared comforting scriptures and led him in prayer, helping him find peace and acceptance.

Strategies for Supporting Patients:

- Active Listening: Allowing patients to express their fears, hopes, and concerns.

- Spiritual Rituals: Providing religious or spiritual rituals that bring comfort and peace.

- Reassurance: Offering words of comfort and reassurance to alleviate fears and anxiety.

Supporting Families

Families of hospice patients often experience anticipatory grief, anxiety, and a sense of helplessness. Chaplains play a crucial role in supporting these families, helping them navigate their emotions, and providing a space for open communication.

Example: Chaplain James and the Thompson Family

The Thompson family was struggling with the impending loss of their father, Mr. Robert Thompson. Chaplain James organized a family meeting, encouraging each member to share their feelings and memories. He provided grief counseling and helped the family understand the dying process. This support enabled the Thompsons to come together and support each other through their shared grief.

Strategies for Supporting Families:

- Family Meetings: Facilitating open discussions where family members can express their emotions and concerns.

- Education: Providing information about the dying process and what to expect.

- Emotional Support: Offering grief counseling and emotional support to help families cope with their feelings.

Bridging the Gap: Facilitating Communication

Effective communication is essential in hospice care. Chaplains often act as mediators, helping to bridge the gap between patients, families, and healthcare providers.

Example: Chaplain Maria and the Lee Family

Mrs. Susan Lee was in her final days, and her family was struggling with how to communicate their love and support. Chaplain Maria facilitated a family meeting, encouraging each member to express their feelings and ask Mrs. Lee any lingering questions. This open dialogue helped the family feel more connected and supported during this difficult time.

Strategies for Facilitating Communication:

- Mediation: Acting as a neutral party to facilitate difficult conversations.

- Encouragement: Encouraging open and honest communication between patients and their families.

- Supportive Presence: Being present during family discussions to offer support and guidance.

Case Study: The Garcia Family

Patient: Mrs. Maria Garcia

Chaplain: David

Mrs. Maria Garcia, a 60-year-old woman with metastatic breast cancer, had a large and loving family. However, the family was experiencing significant stress and emotional turmoil as they faced her impending death.

The Chaplain's Intervention:

Chaplain David recognized the need to support both Mrs. Garcia and her family. He began by spending time with Mrs. Garcia, understanding her spiritual needs and providing her with the sacraments and prayers that were meaningful to her. David also organized a family meeting, where he encouraged each family member to share their thoughts and feelings.

The Grace-Filled Moment:

During one family meeting, David led the family in a group prayer, which brought them together in a moment of shared faith and love. Mrs. Garcia expressed her love and gratitude to her family, and they, in turn, shared their appreciation and support. This moment of unity brought a profound sense of peace and grace to the entire family.

Impact:

David's support helped the Garcia family navigate their emotions and find strength in their unity. Mrs. Garcia's final days were filled with love, faith, and a deep sense of connection, demonstrating the powerful impact of comprehensive spiritual care.

Long-Term Impact: Continuing Support for Families

The support chaplains provide extends beyond the patient's death. They continue to offer grief support and bereavement counseling to families, helping them process their loss and begin the healing journey.

Example: Chaplain Sarah and the Johnson Family

After Mr. Johnson passed away, Chaplain Sarah continued to visit his family, offering grief counseling and emotional support. She helped them plan a memorial service that honored Mr. Johnson's life and provided a space for the family to grieve together. This ongoing support was crucial in helping the Johnson family navigate their grief and find a path forward.

Strategies for Continuing Support:

- Bereavement Counseling: Providing ongoing emotional support and counseling to help families cope with their loss.

- Memorial Services: Assisting families in planning meaningful memorial services.

- Regular Check-Ins: Maintaining contact with families to offer support and resources as they navigate their grief.

Conclusion: The Heart of Shepherding Souls

The dual role of hospice chaplains in supporting both patients and their families is a testament to their dedication and compassion. Through active listening, spiritual guidance, emotional support, and effective communication, chaplains help patients and families find peace and grace in the midst of life's most challenging moments.

As we continue to explore the role of hospice chaplains in the following chapters, the stories and strategies shared here highlight the profound impact of their work. Shepherding souls is a sacred and transformative vocation, bringing light and comfort to those at the end of life and their loved ones.

## LONG-TERM IMPACT

How Chaplains Continue to Influence Families Even After the Patient's Passing

The journey of a hospice chaplain does not end with the passing of a patient. Their role extends into the grief and healing process, providing continuous support and ensuring that families are not left alone in their time of need. This chapter explores how chaplains continue to influence and support families after a patient's death, highlighting the long-term impact of their compassionate care.

Continuing the Journey: The Role of Bereavement Support

After the death of a loved one, families often face a complex and challenging grieving process. Hospice chaplains play a critical role in helping families navigate this journey, offering emotional support, spiritual guidance, and practical resources.

Example: Chaplain Emily and the Johnson Family

Chaplain Emily had been a steady presence for Mr. Johnson and his family throughout his final days. After his passing, she continued to visit the Johnson family, providing a listening ear and offering grief counseling. Emily helped the family plan a memorial service that celebrated Mr. Johnson's life and provided a space for shared mourning. Her ongoing support helped the Johnsons feel connected and supported during their grief.

Key Elements of Bereavement Support:

- Emotional Counseling: Providing one-on-one or group counseling sessions to help families process their grief.

- Memorial Services: Assisting families in planning and conducting meaningful memorial services that honor their loved one.

- Regular Check-Ins: Maintaining contact with families through phone calls, visits, or support groups to offer continued support.

Emotional and Spiritual Healing: Guiding Families Through Grief

Grief is a deeply personal and often isolating experience. Chaplains provide a compassionate presence, helping families find meaning and healing in their loss.

Example: Chaplain James and the Thompson Family

After the passing of Mr. Robert Thompson, Chaplain James continued to support his family. He facilitated a series of grief counseling sessions where family members could share their feelings and memories. James also provided spiritual resources, such as prayers and meditations, that helped the family find solace and peace. His ongoing presence reassured the Thompsons that they were not alone in their grief.

Strategies for Guiding Through Grief:

- Active Listening: Creating a safe space for family members to express their emotions and memories.

- Spiritual Resources: Offering prayers, scriptures, or meditations that provide comfort and hope.

- Personalized Support: Tailoring support to meet the specific needs and preferences of each family.

Building a Community of Support: Bereavement Groups and Resources

Chaplains often facilitate bereavement support groups, bringing together individuals who are experiencing similar losses. These groups provide a sense of community and mutual support.

Example: Chaplain Maria and the Lee Family

Chaplain Maria invited the Lee family to join a bereavement support group she facilitated. The group met weekly, allowing members to share their experiences and support each other. Maria guided the discussions, offering insights and spiritual reflections. The Lee family found comfort in connecting with others who understood their grief, and the support group became a vital part of their healing journey.

Benefits of Bereavement Groups:

- Shared Experience: Providing a space for individuals to connect with others who are going through similar experiences.

- Mutual Support: Encouraging members to support each other, fostering a sense of community and belonging.

- Guided Reflection: Facilitating discussions that help members process their grief and find meaning in their loss.

The Ripple Effect: Long-Term Impact on Families

The influence of hospice chaplains extends far beyond the immediate aftermath of a patient's death. Their compassionate care and support can have lasting effects on families, helping them build resilience and find a path to healing.

Example: Chaplain David and the Garcia Family

Chaplain David continued to support the Garcia family after the passing of Mrs. Maria Garcia. He provided grief counseling and helped the family establish new traditions that honored Mrs. Garcia's memory. Over time, the Garcia family found ways to celebrate her life and keep her spirit alive in their hearts. David's ongoing support helped them navigate their grief and build a foundation for emotional and spiritual healing.

Long-Term Impact:

- Resilience Building: Helping families develop coping strategies and resilience in the face of loss.

- Memorial Traditions: Assisting families in creating lasting traditions that honor their loved one's memory.

- Continued Connection: Providing ongoing support that helps families feel connected and supported as they move forward.

Case Study: The Ongoing Influence of Chaplain Sarah

Patient: Mr. John Thompson

Chaplain: Sarah

Mr. John Thompson, a 70-year-old man with terminal heart disease, had a large family who struggled with the impending loss. Chaplain Sarah provided significant support during his final days, but her influence continued long after his passing.

The Chaplain's Intervention:

Chaplain Sarah organized a series of grief counseling sessions for the Thompson family. She helped them plan a memorial service that celebrated Mr. Thompson's life and facilitated family discussions about their grief and memories. Sarah also introduced the family to a local bereavement support group, where they could connect with others who were experiencing similar losses.

The Grace-Filled Moment:

During a family gathering facilitated by Sarah, each member shared their favorite memories of Mr. Thompson. This gathering became a cherished tradition, helping the family feel connected and supported. The support group also provided ongoing emotional and spiritual support, reinforcing the resilience and unity within the family.

Impact:

Sarah's continued support helped the Thompson family navigate their grief and build a foundation for healing. Her influence extended beyond the immediate loss, fostering long-term resilience and connection within the family.

Conclusion: The Enduring Presence of Hospice Chaplains

The work of hospice chaplains extends far beyond the bedside, continuing to influence and support families long after the passing of a loved one. Through bereavement support, emotional and spiritual healing, community building, and the creation of lasting traditions, chaplains provide a foundation for resilience and healing.

The stories and examples shared in this chapter highlight the profound and lasting impact of hospice chaplains on families. Their compassionate care and continued presence help families navigate the complex journey of grief, ensuring that they are not alone and that their loved ones' memories are honored and cherished. As we continue to explore the role of hospice chaplains in the following chapters, the long-term impact of their work stands as a testament to the enduring power of compassionate, spiritual care.

CHAPTER 06

## SPIRITUAL TOOLS AND PRACTICES

Prayer and Meditation: Different Practices Used by Chaplains to Bring Peace and Comfort

Prayer and meditation are foundational spiritual tools that hospice chaplains use to bring peace, comfort, and a sense of connection to their patients and families. These practices help create a calming environment, provide emotional and spiritual support, and facilitate meaningful moments of reflection. This chapter explores the various ways chaplains incorporate prayer and meditation into their care, highlighting the profound impact these practices can have on the end-of-life experience.

The Power of Prayer

Prayer is a powerful tool that can provide solace, strength, and a sense of connection to a higher power. It is a versatile practice that can be adapted to meet the needs of individuals from diverse faith backgrounds.

Types of Prayer:

- Intercessory Prayer: Praying on behalf of others, asking for divine intervention, comfort, and support.

- Contemplative Prayer: A form of silent prayer focused on being in the presence of the divine, often involving reflection and deep thought.

- Liturgical Prayer: Structured prayers that follow a specific format, often used in religious services and rituals.

- Spontaneous Prayer: Unscripted, heartfelt prayers that respond to the immediate needs and emotions of the moment.

Example: Chaplain Emily and Mr. Johnson

Chaplain Emily used prayer to provide comfort to Mr. Johnson, who was struggling with anxiety and fear about his impending death. She offered spontaneous prayers during their visits, focusing on peace, acceptance, and divine presence. These prayers helped Mr. Johnson feel more at ease and connected to his faith.

Impact:

Prayer can offer immense comfort and a sense of spiritual support. It allows patients to express their hopes, fears, and gratitude, fostering a deeper connection to their faith and to the chaplain.

The Calming Influence of Meditation

Meditation is another powerful spiritual practice that can help patients and families find inner peace, reduce anxiety, and enhance emotional well-being. There are various forms of meditation, each with unique benefits and approaches.

Types of Meditation:

- Mindfulness Meditation: Focusing on the present moment, often through breath awareness or body scans, to cultivate a state of calm and presence.

- Guided Imagery: Using visualization techniques to create peaceful and comforting mental images, often led by the chaplain.

- Loving-Kindness Meditation: Fostering feelings of compassion and love towards oneself and others through specific affirmations and visualizations.

- Transcendental Meditation: A form of silent meditation using a mantra to achieve a deep state of relaxation and awareness.

Example: Chaplain James and Mrs. Lee

Chaplain James introduced mindfulness meditation to Mrs. Lee, who was experiencing significant stress and fear. He guided her through deep breathing exercises and visualization techniques, helping her focus on serene images and positive thoughts. This practice significantly reduced Mrs. Lee's anxiety and helped her find moments of peace.

Impact:

Meditation can profoundly affect emotional and physical well-being, helping patients manage pain, reduce stress, and achieve a sense of tranquility. It also provides a spiritual anchor, allowing patients to explore their inner landscape and find deeper meaning.

Integrating Prayer and Meditation into Care

Chaplains often integrate prayer and meditation into their care routines, creating a holistic approach that addresses the spiritual, emotional, and physical needs of patients and families. This integration can be tailored to individual preferences and cultural backgrounds.

Example: Chaplain Maria and the Garcia Family

Chaplain Maria worked with the Garcia family, who found solace in both prayer and meditation. She led the family in daily prayers, using both liturgical and spontaneous forms. Additionally, Maria introduced guided imagery meditation sessions, helping the family visualize peaceful and comforting scenes. This combination provided a well-rounded spiritual support system for the Garcias.

Strategies for Integration:

- Personalization: Tailoring prayer and meditation practices to the individual's faith, cultural background, and personal preferences.

- Regular Practice: Incorporating these practices into regular visits to establish a routine that brings comfort and stability.

- Education: Teaching patients and families about the benefits and techniques of prayer and meditation, empowering them to continue these practices on their own.

Case Study: The Impact of Combined Practices

Patient: Mr. Ahmed

Chaplain: David

Mr. Ahmed, a devout Muslim, was in his final stages of life and experienced significant anxiety and spiritual distress. Chaplain David recognized the importance of integrating both prayer and meditation to provide holistic support.

The Chaplain's Approach:

David began by leading Mr. Ahmed in traditional Islamic prayers, which provided a familiar and comforting structure. He also introduced mindfulness meditation, focusing on breath awareness and recitations from the Quran. This combination helped Mr. Ahmed connect deeply with his faith while finding moments of peace and calm.

The Grace-Filled Moment:

During one session, as David guided Mr. Ahmed through a meditation focused on the breath and a verse from the Quran, Mr. Ahmed experienced a profound sense of peace. He expressed feeling enveloped by a divine presence and a deep sense of tranquility.

Impact:

The combined practices of prayer and meditation provided Mr. Ahmed with a comprehensive spiritual support system, helping him manage his anxiety and find spiritual fulfillment in his final days.

Practical Tips for Chaplains

Developing a Prayer and Meditation Toolkit:

- Create a Collection of Prayers: Gather prayers from various traditions that can be adapted to different situations and preferences.

- Learn Meditation Techniques: Study various forms of meditation to offer a range of practices tailored to individual needs.

- Build a Calming Environment: Use soft lighting, calming sounds, and comfortable seating to create a conducive environment for prayer and meditation.

Engaging with Patients and Families:

- Assess Needs and Preferences: Understand the spiritual and emotional needs of patients and families to provide appropriate practices.

- Be Flexible and Adaptable: Be willing to adjust practices based on feedback and changing needs.

- Provide Resources: Offer books, recordings, or written guides on prayer and meditation to encourage continued practice.

Conclusion: The Transformative Power of Prayer and Meditation

Prayer and meditation are powerful spiritual tools that hospice chaplains use to bring peace, comfort, and spiritual connection to patients and families. These practices help create a calming environment, provide emotional and spiritual support, and facilitate meaningful moments of reflection. By integrating prayer and meditation into their care, chaplains offer a holistic approach that addresses the diverse needs of those they serve.

The stories and examples shared in this chapter highlight the profound impact of these practices, demonstrating how prayer and meditation can transform the end-of-life experience. As we continue to explore the role of hospice chaplains in the following chapters, the power of prayer and meditation stands as a testament to the essential nature of spiritual care in providing peace and comfort to those at the end of life.

## HOW CHAPLAINS CONTINUE TO INFLUENCE FAMILIES EVEN AFTER THE PATIENT'S PASSING

The role of a hospice chaplain extends far beyond the bedside of a dying patient. Their influence persists long after the patient has passed, providing crucial support to families as they navigate the often tumultuous journey of grief and loss. This chapter explores the long-term impact that chaplains have on families, highlighting the enduring nature of their support and the transformative effect it can have on the grieving process.

Continuing the Journey: Bereavement Support

Grief does not end with the funeral; in many ways, it begins in earnest after the loved one has been laid to rest. Chaplains recognize this and remain a vital source of support for families during the bereavement period.

Example: Chaplain Emily and the Johnson Family

Chaplain Emily had been a constant presence for the Johnson family during Mr. Johnson's illness. After his passing, she continued to visit the family, offering a listening ear and grief counseling. Emily helped the family plan a memorial service that celebrated Mr. Johnson's life, providing a space for shared mourning and remembrance.

Key Elements of Bereavement Support:

- Emotional Counseling: Providing individual or group counseling sessions to help families process their grief.

- Memorial Services: Assisting families in planning and conducting meaningful memorial services.

- Regular Check-Ins: Maintaining contact with families through phone calls, visits, or support groups to offer continued support.

Emotional and Spiritual Healing: Guiding Families Through Grief

Grief is a deeply personal and often isolating experience. Chaplains offer a compassionate presence, helping families find meaning and healing in their loss.

Example: Chaplain James and the Thompson Family

After the passing of Mr. Robert Thompson, Chaplain James continued to support his family. He facilitated a series of grief counseling sessions where family members could share their feelings and memories. James also provided spiritual resources, such as prayers and meditations, that helped the family find solace and peace. His ongoing presence reassured the Thompsons that they were not alone in their grief.

Strategies for Guiding Through Grief:

- Active Listening: Creating a safe space for family members to express their emotions and memories.

- Spiritual Resources: Offering prayers, scriptures, or meditations that provide comfort and hope.

- Personalized Support: Tailoring support to meet the specific needs and preferences of each family.

Building a Community of Support: Bereavement Groups and Resources

Chaplains often facilitate bereavement support groups, bringing together individuals who are experiencing similar losses. These groups provide a sense of community and mutual support.

Example: Chaplain Maria and the Lee Family

Chaplain Maria invited the Lee family to join a bereavement support group she facilitated. The group met weekly, allowing members to share their experiences and support each other. Maria guided the discussions, offering insights and spiritual reflections. The Lee family found comfort in connecting with others who understood their grief, and the support group became a vital part of their healing journey.

Benefits of Bereavement Groups:

- Shared Experience: Providing a space for individuals to connect with others who are going through similar experiences.

- Mutual Support: Encouraging members to support each other, fostering a sense of community and belonging.

- Guided Reflection: Facilitating discussions that help members process their grief and find meaning in their loss.

The Ripple Effect: Long-Term Impact on Families

The influence of hospice chaplains extends far beyond the immediate aftermath of a patient's death. Their compassionate care and support can have lasting effects on families, helping them build resilience and find a path to healing.

Example: Chaplain David and the Garcia Family

Chaplain David continued to support the Garcia family after the passing of Mrs. Maria Garcia. He provided grief counseling and helped the family establish new traditions that honored Mrs. Garcia's memory. Over time, the Garcia family found ways to celebrate her life and keep her spirit alive in their hearts. David's ongoing support helped them navigate their grief and build a foundation for emotional and spiritual healing.

Long-Term Impact:

- Resilience Building: Helping families develop coping strategies and resilience in the face of loss.

- Memorial Traditions: Assisting families in creating lasting traditions that honor their loved one's memory.

- Continued Connection: Providing ongoing support that helps families feel connected and supported as they move forward.

Case Study: The Ongoing Influence of Chaplain Sarah

Patient: Mr. John Thompson

Chaplain: Sarah

Mr. John Thompson, a 70-year-old man with terminal heart disease, had a large family who struggled with the impending loss. Chaplain Sarah provided significant support during his final days, but her influence continued long after his passing.

The Chaplain's Intervention:

Chaplain Sarah organized a series of grief counseling sessions for the Thompson family. She helped them plan a memorial service that celebrated Mr. Thompson's life and facilitated family discussions about their grief and memories. Sarah also introduced the family to a local bereavement support group, where they could connect with others who were experiencing similar losses.

The Grace-Filled Moment:

During a family gathering facilitated by Sarah, each member shared their favorite memories of Mr. Thompson. This gathering became a cherished tradition, helping the family feel connected and supported. The support group also provided ongoing emotional and spiritual support, reinforcing the resilience and unity within the family.

Impact:

Sarah's continued support helped the Thompson family navigate their grief and build a foundation for healing. Her influence extended beyond the immediate loss, fostering long-term resilience and connection within the family.

Practical Strategies for Chaplains

Developing Long-Term Support Plans:

- Regular Follow-Ups: Schedule regular check-ins with families to offer ongoing support and address any emerging needs.

- Resource Provision: Provide families with resources such as books, support group information, and contact lists for additional counseling services.

- Personalized Care Plans: Tailor support plans to the specific needs and preferences of each family, ensuring that care continues to be relevant and effective.

Engaging with Families:

- Active Engagement: Maintain an active role in families' lives through regular communication and visits.

- Empathy and Compassion: Approach each interaction with empathy and compassion, acknowledging the unique journey of each family.

- Building Trust: Foster a relationship of trust and openness, encouraging families to share their feelings and seek support as needed.

Conclusion: The Enduring Presence of Hospice Chaplains

The work of hospice chaplains extends far beyond the bedside, continuing to influence and support families long after the passing of a loved one. Through bereavement support, emotional and spiritual healing, community building, and the creation of lasting traditions, chaplains provide a foundation for resilience and healing.

The stories and examples shared in this chapter highlight the profound and lasting impact of hospice chaplains on families. Their compassionate care and continued presence help families navigate the complex journey of grief, ensuring that they are not alone and that their loved ones' memories are honored and cherished. As we continue to explore the role of hospice chaplains in the following chapters, the long-term impact of their work stands as a testament to the enduring power of compassionate, spiritual care.

---

# CHAPTER 07

# INTERFAITH AND MULTICULTURAL APPROACHES

Respecting Diverse Beliefs: Providing Spiritual Care in a Multicultural and Multi-Faith Context

In an increasingly globalized world, hospice chaplains often encounter patients and families from diverse cultural and religious backgrounds. Providing spiritual care in such a context requires sensitivity, understanding, and respect for a wide range of beliefs and practices. This chapter explores the approaches chaplains use to honor and integrate diverse spiritual traditions into their care, highlighting the importance of cultural competence and interfaith dialogue.

Understanding Cultural Competence

Cultural competence involves recognizing, respecting, and valuing the diverse beliefs and practices of patients and families. It requires chaplains to be aware of their own cultural biases and to engage in continuous learning about other cultures and faiths.

Key Elements of Cultural Competence:

- Self-Awareness: Understanding one's own cultural background and biases.

- Cultural Knowledge: Gaining knowledge about different cultures, religions, and spiritual practices.

- Cultural Skills: Developing the ability to communicate and interact effectively with people from different cultural backgrounds.

- Cultural Encounters: Engaging in interactions with individuals from diverse backgrounds to enhance understanding and empathy.

Respecting and Honoring Diverse Beliefs

Providing spiritual care in a multicultural context involves respecting and honoring the unique beliefs and practices of each patient and their family. Chaplains must be flexible and open-minded, adapting their approach to meet the specific needs of those they serve.

Example: Chaplain Emily and Mr. Singh

Mr. Singh, a 70-year-old man with terminal cancer, was a devout Sikh. Chaplain Emily took the time to learn about Sikhism and consulted with Mr. Singh and his family about their spiritual needs. She respected their practices, such as daily prayers and the use of a specific prayer book. Emily also arranged for a local Sikh priest to visit Mr. Singh, providing him with the spiritual support he needed.

Strategies for Respecting Diverse Beliefs:

- Active Listening: Listening carefully to patients and families to understand their beliefs and practices.

- Education: Learning about the religious and cultural backgrounds of patients to provide informed care.

- Collaboration: Working with religious leaders and community members to ensure that spiritual needs are met.

Providing Inclusive Spiritual Care

Inclusive spiritual care involves creating an environment where all beliefs are respected and valued. Chaplains can foster inclusivity by incorporating a variety of spiritual practices and rituals into their care.

Example: Chaplain James and Mrs. Chen

Mrs. Chen, a 65-year-old woman with advanced heart disease, practiced Buddhism. Chaplain James incorporated elements of Buddhist practice, such as meditation and chanting, into his visits. He also respected Mrs. Chen's dietary restrictions and provided a quiet space for her to practice her rituals. This inclusive approach helped Mrs. Chen feel supported and respected in her spiritual journey.

Strategies for Providing Inclusive Spiritual Care:

- Flexibility: Being open to incorporating different spiritual practices and rituals into care.

- Adaptation: Tailoring spiritual care to meet the specific needs and preferences of each patient.

- Inclusivity: Creating an environment where all beliefs are respected and valued.

Case Study: Interfaith Dialogue and Support

Patient: Mr. Ahmed

Chaplain: Maria

Mr. Ahmed, a 75-year-old Muslim man, was in the final stages of life. His family was deeply religious, and they wanted to ensure that his spiritual needs were met according to Islamic traditions.

The Chaplain's Approach:

Chaplain Maria, who had experience with interfaith dialogue, took the time to learn about Islamic practices and consulted with Mr. Ahmed's family. She arranged for an imam to visit Mr. Ahmed regularly and respected their request for daily prayers and specific dietary restrictions. Maria also facilitated conversations between the healthcare team and the family to ensure that all cultural and religious needs were honored.

The Grace-Filled Moment:

During one of her visits, Maria participated in a prayer session with Mr. Ahmed's family, respecting their traditions and joining in the spiritual practice. This moment of shared faith and mutual respect brought immense comfort to Mr. Ahmed and his family, highlighting the importance of honoring diverse beliefs in spiritual care.

Impact:

Maria's respectful and inclusive approach helped Mr. Ahmed and his family feel supported and valued. Her willingness to engage in interfaith dialogue and adapt her care to meet their needs fostered a sense of trust and comfort.

Building Relationships with Religious Leaders

Chaplains can enhance their ability to provide inclusive spiritual care by building relationships with local religious leaders and communities. These connections can provide valuable resources and support for patients and families from diverse backgrounds.

Example: Chaplain David and the Garcia Family

The Garcia family, who were practicing Catholics, wanted to ensure that their spiritual needs were met during their mother's final days. Chaplain David built a relationship with the local Catholic church and arranged for a priest to visit regularly. He also coordinated the sacraments and rituals that were important to the family, ensuring that their spiritual needs were fully supported.

Strategies for Building Relationships:

- Networking: Connecting with local religious leaders and communities to build a network of support.

- Collaboration: Working collaboratively with religious leaders to provide comprehensive spiritual care.

- Resource Sharing: Sharing resources and information to enhance the spiritual care provided to patients and families.

Practical Tips for Chaplains

Developing Cultural Competence:

- Ongoing Education: Participate in cultural competence training and education programs.

- Reading and Research: Read books and articles about different cultures and religions to enhance your knowledge.

- Community Engagement: Engage with diverse communities to learn about their practices and beliefs firsthand.

Providing Inclusive Spiritual Care:

- Ask and Listen: Always ask patients and families about their spiritual needs and preferences, and listen carefully to their responses.

- Be Flexible: Be willing to adapt your approach to meet the specific needs of each patient.

- Show Respect: Show respect for all beliefs and practices, even if they differ from your own.

Conclusion: The Importance of Interfaith and Multicultural Approaches

Providing spiritual care in a multicultural and multi-faith context is a vital aspect of hospice chaplaincy. By respecting and honoring diverse beliefs, chaplains can create an inclusive environment where all patients and families feel valued and supported. The stories and examples shared in this chapter highlight the profound impact of cultural competence and interfaith dialogue, demonstrating how chaplains can provide compassionate and effective care in a diverse world.

As we continue to explore the role of hospice chaplains in the following chapters, the importance of respecting diverse beliefs stands as a testament to the essential nature of inclusive, culturally competent care. By embracing and honoring the rich tapestry of human spirituality, chaplains can bring peace, comfort, and a sense of belonging to those at the end of life and their loved ones.

# INCLUSIVE PRACTICES

Strategies for Addressing the Spiritual Needs of Patients from Various Religious Backgrounds

In a multicultural and multi-faith society, hospice chaplains often encounter patients and families from diverse religious traditions. Addressing the spiritual needs of these patients requires sensitivity, knowledge, and a commitment to inclusivity. This chapter explores inclusive practices and strategies that chaplains can use to provide respectful and effective spiritual care to individuals from various religious backgrounds.

Understanding the Importance of Inclusivity

Inclusivity in spiritual care means recognizing and respecting the unique beliefs, practices, and needs of each patient. It involves creating an environment where all individuals feel valued and supported in their spiritual journey, regardless of their faith tradition.

Key Elements of Inclusivity:

- Respect: Honoring the beliefs and practices of all patients.

- Flexibility: Adapting care practices to meet the diverse needs of patients.

- Collaboration: Working with patients, families, and religious leaders to ensure comprehensive spiritual support.

Strategies for Inclusive Spiritual Care

To provide inclusive spiritual care, chaplains can employ various strategies that address the unique needs of patients from different religious backgrounds. These strategies involve active listening, cultural competence, and collaboration with religious leaders and communities.

1. Active Listening and Assessment

Active listening is a fundamental skill for chaplains, enabling them to understand the specific spiritual needs and preferences of each patient.

Example: Chaplain Emily and Mr. Singh

Mr. Singh, a devout Sikh, expressed a need for specific prayers and rituals during his final days. Chaplain Emily took the time to listen to Mr. Singh and his family, understanding their spiritual needs and preferences. She used this information to provide tailored spiritual support that respected their Sikh traditions.

Strategies for Active Listening and Assessment:

- Open-Ended Questions: Ask open-ended questions to encourage patients and families to share their beliefs and needs.

- Non-Judgmental Listening: Listen without judgment, allowing patients to express their spirituality freely.

- Documentation: Document the spiritual needs and preferences of each patient to ensure consistent and personalized care.

2. Cultural Competence and Education

Cultural competence involves understanding and respecting the diverse cultural and religious backgrounds of patients. This requires ongoing education and a willingness to learn about different traditions.

Example: Chaplain James and Mrs. Lee

Mrs. Lee, a practicing Buddhist, had specific spiritual needs related to her faith. Chaplain James educated himself about Buddhism, learning about meditation practices, chanting, and dietary restrictions. This knowledge allowed him to provide informed and respectful spiritual care to Mrs. Lee.

Strategies for Cultural Competence and Education:

- Ongoing Training: Participate in cultural competence training programs and workshops.

- Reading and Research: Read books, articles, and resources about different religions and cultural practices.

- Community Engagement: Engage with diverse religious communities to learn about their beliefs and practices firsthand.

3. Collaboration with Religious Leaders

Collaborating with local religious leaders can enhance the spiritual care provided to patients. These leaders can offer valuable insights, support, and resources.

Example: Chaplain Maria and Mr. Ahmed

Mr. Ahmed, a Muslim patient, required specific religious support. Chaplain Maria collaborated with a local imam to ensure that Mr. Ahmed received the appropriate spiritual care, including prayers and rituals. This collaboration provided Mr. Ahmed with the spiritual comfort he needed.

Strategies for Collaboration with Religious Leaders:

- Networking: Build relationships with local religious leaders and communities.

- Consultation: Consult with religious leaders to understand the specific needs of patients from their faith traditions.

- Resource Sharing: Share resources and information to enhance the spiritual care provided to patients.

4. Incorporating Diverse Spiritual Practices

Incorporating diverse spiritual practices into care can help meet the unique needs of each patient. Chaplains can use various rituals, prayers, and meditations to provide comprehensive spiritual support.

Example: Chaplain David and the Garcia Family

The Garcia family, practicing Catholics, wanted to ensure that their spiritual needs were met. Chaplain David incorporated Catholic practices such as the Rosary, Holy Communion, and anointing of the sick into his care. This inclusive approach provided the Garcia family with the spiritual support they needed.

Strategies for Incorporating Diverse Spiritual Practices:

- Flexibility: Be open to incorporating different spiritual practices and rituals into care.

- Adaptation: Tailor spiritual practices to meet the specific needs and preferences of each patient.

- Inclusivity: Create an environment where all spiritual practices are respected and valued.

5. Creating a Sacred Space

Creating a sacred space can provide a comforting and spiritually supportive environment for patients. This space can be adapted to reflect the patient's religious and cultural background.

Example: Chaplain Sarah and Mrs. Thompson

Mrs. Thompson, a devout Hindu, found comfort in having a sacred space in her room. Chaplain Sarah helped create this space by setting up a small altar with a statue of a deity, flowers, and a prayer book. This sacred space provided Mrs. Thompson with a sense of peace and spiritual connection.

Strategies for Creating a Sacred Space:

- Personalization: Personalize the sacred space to reflect the patient's beliefs and practices.

- Simplicity: Keep the space simple and focused on the elements that are most meaningful to the patient.

- Accessibility: Ensure that the sacred space is easily accessible to the patient and their family.

Case Study: Inclusive Spiritual Care for a Multicultural Family

Patient: Mr. Chen

Chaplain: Emily

Mr. Chen, a 68-year-old man with terminal lung cancer, came from a multicultural family. His wife was Christian, while he identified as a Taoist. Their children practiced a blend of both traditions.

The Chaplain's Approach:

Chaplain Emily recognized the importance of honoring both traditions. She engaged in active listening with

Mr. Chen and his family to understand their spiritual needs. Emily collaborated with a Taoist priest to provide specific rituals for Mr. Chen, while also incorporating Christian prayers and hymns for his wife. She created a sacred space in Mr. Chen's room that included elements from both traditions, ensuring that all family members felt supported.

The Grace-Filled Moment:

During one visit, Emily facilitated a family prayer session where each member shared their beliefs and offered prayers in their own tradition. This moment of shared spirituality and mutual respect brought immense comfort to Mr. Chen and his family.

Impact:

Emily's inclusive approach helped Mr. Chen and his family feel respected and supported. Her ability to honor and integrate diverse spiritual practices fostered a sense of unity and peace, demonstrating the profound impact of inclusive spiritual care.

Practical Tips for Chaplains

Developing Inclusive Practices:

- Ask and Listen: Always ask patients and families about their spiritual needs and preferences, and listen carefully to their responses.

- Be Flexible: Be willing to adapt your approach to meet the specific needs of each patient.

- Show Respect: Show respect for all beliefs and practices, even if they differ from your own.

Enhancing Cultural Competence:

- Ongoing Education: Participate in cultural competence training and education programs.

- Reading and Research: Read books and articles about different cultures and religions to enhance your knowledge.

- Community Engagement: Engage with diverse communities to learn about their practices and beliefs firsthand.

Building Relationships with Religious Leaders:

- Networking: Connect with local religious leaders and communities to build a network of support.

- Collaboration: Work collaboratively with religious leaders to provide comprehensive spiritual care.

- Resource Sharing: Share resources and information to enhance the spiritual care provided to patients.

Conclusion: The Power of Inclusive Spiritual Care

Inclusive spiritual care is essential in a multicultural and multi-faith society. By respecting and honoring diverse beliefs, chaplains can create an environment where all patients and families feel valued and supported. The strategies and examples shared in this chapter highlight the importance of cultural competence, collaboration, and flexibility in providing effective spiritual care.

As we continue to explore the role of hospice chaplains in the following chapters, the importance of inclusive practices stands as a testament to the essential nature of compassionate, respectful, and culturally competent care. By embracing and honoring the rich tapestry of human spirituality, chaplains can bring peace, comfort, and a sense of belonging to those at the end of life and their loved ones.

CHAPTER 08

# CHALLENGES AND ETHICAL DILEMMAS

Navigating Difficult Situations: Common Challenges Faced by Hospice Chaplains

Hospice chaplains play a critical role in providing spiritual care to patients and families during the end-of-life journey. This work, while deeply rewarding, is fraught with challenges and ethical dilemmas that require a delicate balance of empathy, wisdom, and professional ethics. This chapter explores some of the common challenges faced by hospice chaplains, highlighting the ethical dilemmas and emotional strain inherent in their vocation.

Ethical Dilemmas in Hospice Chaplaincy

Ethical dilemmas often arise in hospice care, requiring chaplains to navigate complex situations with sensitivity and integrity. These dilemmas can involve conflicts between patients' wishes, family members' desires, and medical recommendations.

1. Respecting Autonomy vs. Beneficence

Chaplains often face the challenge of balancing respect for a patient's autonomy with the principle of beneficence, which involves acting in the patient's best interest.

Example: Chaplain Emily and Mr. Johnson

Mr. Johnson, a terminally ill patient, expressed a desire to stop all medical treatments and focus on comfort care. His family, however, wanted him to continue aggressive treatments. Chaplain Emily faced the ethical dilemma of respecting Mr. Johnson's autonomy while considering the family's distress.

Navigating the Dilemma:

Emily facilitated a family meeting where Mr. Johnson could articulate his wishes. She provided emotional support to the family, helping them understand his perspective and the importance of honoring his autonomy. Emily's compassionate mediation helped the family come to terms with Mr. Johnson's decision, ultimately respecting his autonomy while supporting the family's emotional needs.

2. Confidentiality vs. Family Involvement

Maintaining confidentiality while involving family members in care decisions can be challenging, especially when there are conflicting interests or lack of consensus among family members.

Example: Chaplain James and Mrs. Lee

Mrs. Lee confided in Chaplain James about her wish to reconcile with an estranged son before her death but asked James to keep this information confidential from her other children. James faced the ethical dilemma of maintaining confidentiality while recognizing the family's need for open communication.

Navigating the Dilemma:

James respected Mrs. Lee's confidentiality, but he gently encouraged her to share her wishes with her other children. He offered to facilitate the conversation, ensuring a supportive environment. This approach honored Mrs. Lee's confidentiality while promoting family involvement and reconciliation.

3. Truth-Telling vs. Protecting Hope

Balancing the need for honest communication with the desire to maintain hope is a common ethical challenge. Patients and families may struggle with the harsh realities of terminal illness, and chaplains must navigate this delicate terrain.

Example: Chaplain Maria and Mr. Ahmed

Mr. Ahmed's family wanted to shield him from the full extent of his prognosis, hoping to maintain his spirits. However, Mr. Ahmed sought honest answers about his condition. Chaplain Maria faced the ethical dilemma of truth-telling versus protecting hope.

Navigating the Dilemma:

Maria engaged in open and honest conversations with Mr. Ahmed, providing the information he sought while offering emotional support. She also worked with the family to help them understand the importance of respecting Mr. Ahmed's need for truth. By fostering open communication, Maria helped maintain hope while honoring Mr. Ahmed's desire for honesty.

Emotional Strain and Self-Care

The emotional strain of hospice chaplaincy can be significant, as chaplains regularly confront death, grief, and suffering. Managing this emotional toll requires intentional self-care and professional support.

1. Compassion Fatigue and Burnout

Compassion fatigue and burnout are common risks for hospice chaplains, stemming from the constant exposure to emotional pain and suffering.

Example: Chaplain David's Experience

Chaplain David, who had been supporting multiple families through intense grief, began experiencing symptoms of burnout, such as emotional exhaustion and decreased empathy. Recognizing these signs, David sought support from his supervisor and engaged in self-care practices.

Strategies for Managing Compassion Fatigue and Burnout:

- Professional Supervision: Regular supervision sessions provide a space to discuss challenging cases and receive guidance.

- Peer Support: Engaging with fellow chaplains in support groups can offer mutual understanding and encouragement.

- Personal Self-Care: Practicing self-care activities such as exercise, hobbies, and spiritual practices helps maintain emotional well-being.

2. Emotional Boundaries

Maintaining emotional boundaries while providing compassionate care is essential to prevent emotional overload and maintain professional integrity.

Example: Chaplain Sarah and the Thompson Family

Chaplain Sarah developed a close bond with the Thompson family during Mr. Thompson's illness. After his passing, Sarah found herself deeply affected by their grief. She recognized the need to maintain emotional boundaries to provide effective support.

Strategies for Maintaining Emotional Boundaries:

- Reflection and Supervision: Regular reflection and supervision help chaplains process their emotions and maintain professional boundaries.

- Mindfulness Practices: Mindfulness techniques can help chaplains stay present and centered, preventing emotional entanglement.

- Clear Communication: Setting clear boundaries with families while expressing empathy and support ensures a balanced approach to care.

Case Study: Navigating Ethical Dilemmas and Emotional Strain

Patient: Mrs. Garcia

Chaplain: Maria

Mrs. Garcia, a 60-year-old woman with metastatic breast cancer, was nearing the end of her life. Her family struggled with accepting her prognosis and wished to pursue aggressive treatments, despite Mrs. Garcia's desire for comfort care. Chaplain Maria faced the ethical dilemma of respecting Mrs. Garcia's wishes while addressing the family's hopes.

The Chaplain's Approach:

Maria facilitated a family meeting, creating a safe space for open communication. She gently encouraged Mrs. Garcia to express her wishes and provided emotional support to the family as they processed her decision. Maria also sought guidance from her supervisor to navigate the complex emotions involved.

The Grace-Filled Moment:

Through compassionate mediation, Maria helped the family understand the importance of honoring Mrs. Garcia's wishes. This process brought a sense of peace to Mrs. Garcia and allowed the family to support her in her final days, ultimately respecting her autonomy and addressing the ethical dilemma.

Impact:

Maria's approach helped navigate the ethical dilemma and emotional strain, providing a compassionate and respectful resolution. Her ability to balance empathy with professional boundaries ensured effective and supportive care. Practical Tips for Chaplains

Navigating Ethical Dilemmas:

- Seek Guidance: Consult with supervisors or ethics committees when faced with complex dilemmas.

- Facilitate Open Communication: Encourage open and honest conversations between patients and families to address conflicting needs and wishes.

- Document Decisions: Documenting ethical decisions and the reasoning behind them can provide clarity and accountability.

Managing Emotional Strain:

- Regular Self-Reflection: Engage in regular self-reflection to understand and manage emotional responses.

- Professional Support: Seek support from supervisors, peer groups, or counselors to process challenging emotions.

- Establish Rituals: Create personal rituals or practices that help transition between work and personal life, maintaining a healthy balance.

Conclusion: The Resilience of Hospice Chaplains

The challenges and ethical dilemmas faced by hospice chaplains are significant, requiring a balance of empathy, wisdom, and professional integrity. By navigating these difficulties with compassion and resilience, chaplains provide essential support to patients and families during the end-of-life journey.

The strategies and examples shared in this chapter highlight the importance of ethical decision-making, emotional self-care, and professional support in hospice chaplaincy. As we continue to explore the role of hospice chaplains in the following chapters, the resilience and dedication of these professionals stand as a testament to their crucial role in providing compassionate, ethical, and effective spiritual care.

## PROFESSIONAL BOUNDARIES

Maintaining Professional Boundaries While Providing Compassionate Care

Maintaining professional boundaries is a crucial aspect of hospice chaplaincy. It ensures that chaplains can provide compassionate, effective care without becoming overwhelmed or compromising their professional integrity. This chapter explores the importance of professional boundaries, common boundary challenges, and strategies for maintaining a healthy balance between compassion and professionalism.

Understanding Professional Boundaries

Professional boundaries define the limits of appropriate behavior and interactions between chaplains and their patients or families. These boundaries help protect both the chaplain and those they serve, ensuring that care remains effective and ethically sound.

Key Elements of Professional Boundaries:

- Emotional Boundaries: Managing personal emotions to avoid becoming overly attached or emotionally entangled with patients and families.

- Time Boundaries: Setting limits on the amount of time spent with patients and families to prevent burnout and maintain a balanced workload.

- Role Boundaries: Clearly defining the chaplain's role to avoid overstepping into areas best handled by other professionals, such as medical or social work staff.

Common Boundary Challenges

Hospice chaplains often face situations that test their professional boundaries. Recognizing and addressing these challenges is essential for maintaining effective and ethical care.

1. Emotional Attachment

Developing a strong emotional bond with patients and families is natural, but excessive attachment can lead to emotional burnout and impaired judgment.

Example: Chaplain Emily and Mr. Johnson

Chaplain Emily developed a close relationship with Mr. Johnson and his family during his illness. After Mr. Johnson's passing, Emily found herself deeply affected by the family's grief, struggling to maintain her emotional equilibrium.

Navigating the Challenge:

Emily sought support from her supervisor and engaged in regular self-reflection to process her emotions. She practiced mindfulness techniques to stay present and centered, allowing her to provide compassionate care without becoming overwhelmed.

Strategies for Managing Emotional Attachment:

- Regular Supervision: Engage in supervision or counseling to discuss emotional challenges and receive guidance.

- Mindfulness Practices: Practice mindfulness to remain present and maintain emotional balance.

- Self-Reflection: Regularly reflect on emotional responses to understand and manage them effectively.

2. Over-Involvement

Becoming too involved in the personal lives of patients and families can blur the lines between professional and personal relationships, potentially compromising the chaplain's objectivity and effectiveness.

Example: Chaplain James and Mrs. Lee

Chaplain James found himself becoming increasingly involved in Mrs. Lee's family dynamics, often acting as a mediator in family disputes. This over-involvement began to affect his ability to provide impartial spiritual care.

Navigating the Challenge:

James set clear boundaries with Mrs. Lee's family, focusing on his role as a spiritual support rather than a mediator. He referred the family to a social worker for ongoing mediation and family counseling, ensuring that his care remained focused on spiritual support.

Strategies for Managing Over-Involvement:

- Clear Role Definition: Clearly define and communicate your role as a chaplain to patients and families.

- Referrals: Refer patients and families to appropriate professionals for issues outside the scope of spiritual care.

- Boundary Setting: Set and maintain clear boundaries around the extent of your involvement in patients' personal lives.

3. Time Management

Spending excessive time with a single patient or family can lead to burnout and neglect of other patients' needs. Balancing time effectively is crucial for providing equitable care.

Example: Chaplain Maria and Mr. Ahmed

Chaplain Maria spent a significant amount of time with Mr. Ahmed and his family, who were experiencing intense grief and spiritual distress. This focus began to affect her ability to attend to other patients' needs.

Navigating the Challenge:

Maria created a balanced schedule that allocated time equitably among her patients. She communicated her availability clearly to Mr. Ahmed's family and arranged for additional support from other members of the hospice care team.

Strategies for Managing Time:

- Scheduling: Create a balanced schedule that ensures equitable time for all patients.

- Clear Communication: Communicate your availability and time constraints clearly to patients and families.

- Delegation: Delegate tasks and involve other team members to provide comprehensive support.

Maintaining Professional Boundaries: Best Practices

Maintaining professional boundaries requires intentional practices and a commitment to self-care and professional ethics. Here are some best practices for hospice chaplains:

1. Regular Supervision and Peer Support

Engaging in regular supervision and peer support provides a space to discuss boundary challenges and receive guidance from experienced colleagues.

Example: Chaplain David's Peer Support Group

Chaplain David participated in a monthly peer support group with other hospice chaplains. This group provided a safe space to discuss challenging cases, share experiences, and receive feedback on maintaining professional boundaries.

Benefits of Supervision and Peer Support:

- Perspective: Gaining new perspectives and insights from colleagues.

- Support: Receiving emotional and professional support.

- Accountability: Ensuring accountability for maintaining professional boundaries.

2. Self-Care and Wellness Practices

Practicing self-care and wellness is essential for managing emotional strain and maintaining professional boundaries.

Example: Chaplain Sarah's Self-Care Routine

Chaplain Sarah developed a self-care routine that included regular exercise, meditation, and time spent with loved ones. This routine helped her manage stress and maintain emotional balance.

Strategies for Self-Care and Wellness:

- Regular Exercise: Engage in regular physical activity to manage stress and maintain physical health.

- Mindfulness and Meditation: Practice mindfulness and meditation to stay centered and balanced.

- Social Support: Spend time with family and friends to nurture personal relationships and well-being.

3. Clear Communication and Documentation

Clear communication and thorough documentation help maintain professional boundaries and ensure transparent and ethical care.

Example: Chaplain Emily's Documentation Practices

Chaplain Emily maintained detailed records of her interactions with patients and families. She documented spiritual assessments, care plans, and any boundary challenges that arose, ensuring accountability and clarity.

Benefits of Clear Communication and Documentation:

- Transparency: Ensuring transparency in care practices.

- Accountability: Providing a record of interactions and decisions.

- Clarity: Maintaining clarity in roles and responsibilities.

Case Study: Navigating Professional Boundaries

Patient: Mrs. Garcia

Chaplain: Maria

Mrs. Garcia, a 60-year-old woman with metastatic breast cancer, had a large and emotionally involved family. Chaplain Maria provided spiritual support to Mrs. Garcia and her family, but she found herself becoming deeply involved in their personal dynamics.

The Chaplain's Approach:

Maria recognized the need to maintain professional boundaries to provide effective care. She set clear limits on her involvement in family disputes and focused on her role as a spiritual support. Maria referred the family to a social worker for ongoing mediation and counseling, ensuring that her care remained centered on spiritual needs.

The Grace-Filled Moment:

By maintaining clear boundaries, Maria was able to provide consistent and effective spiritual support to Mrs. Garcia and her family. Her approach helped the family navigate their grief while preserving her professional integrity and emotional well-being.

Impact:

Maria's ability to navigate professional boundaries ensured that she could provide compassionate care without becoming overwhelmed or compromising her effectiveness. Her approach demonstrated the importance of clear boundaries in maintaining ethical and effective spiritual care.

Practical Tips for Chaplains

Maintaining Professional Boundaries:

- Regular Supervision: Engage in regular supervision to discuss boundary challenges and receive guidance.

- Self-Care Practices: Develop and maintain a self-care routine to manage stress and emotional strain.

- Clear Communication: Communicate your role and boundaries clearly to patients and families.

- Thorough Documentation: Document interactions and decisions to ensure transparency and accountability.

Navigating Emotional Challenges:

- Mindfulness Practices: Practice mindfulness to stay present and balanced.

- Peer Support: Participate in peer support groups to share experiences and receive feedback.

- Professional Development: Engage in ongoing professional development to enhance skills and knowledge.

Conclusion: The Balance of Compassion and Professionalism

Maintaining professional boundaries is essential for hospice chaplains to provide compassionate and effective care. By navigating boundary challenges with empathy and integrity, chaplains can support patients and families while preserving their professional and emotional well-being.

The strategies and examples shared in this chapter highlight the importance of clear boundaries, self-care, and professional support in hospice chaplaincy. As we continue to explore the role of hospice chaplains in the following chapters, the balance of compassion and professionalism stands as a testament to their crucial role in providing ethical, effective, and compassionate spiritual care.

CHAPTER 09

## TRAINING AND DEVELOPMENT

Educational Pathways: Required Education and Training for Aspiring Hospice Chaplains

Aspiring hospice chaplains require a comprehensive and multidisciplinary education to prepare for the complex and sensitive nature of their work. This chapter outlines the educational pathways, training programs, and necessary qualifications for those who feel called to this sacred vocation. It also highlights the importance of ongoing professional development to ensure that chaplains remain effective and compassionate in their roles.

Formal Education Requirements

The journey to becoming a hospice chaplain typically begins with formal education in theology, pastoral care, or a related field. This foundational education provides the essential knowledge and skills needed to offer spiritual support and navigate the complexities of end-of-life care.

1. Bachelor's Degree

Most aspiring chaplains start with a bachelor's degree in a relevant field such as theology, religious studies, psychology, or social work. This undergraduate education provides a broad understanding of religious traditions, human behavior, and counseling techniques.

Key Areas of Study:

- Theology and Religious Studies: Understanding the core beliefs and practices of various religious traditions.

- Psychology: Learning about human behavior, mental health, and emotional support.

- Counseling: Developing basic counseling skills and techniques.

Example: Bachelor's Program

Jane, an aspiring chaplain, completed a bachelor's degree in religious studies. Her coursework included classes on world religions, pastoral counseling, and psychology. This education provided her with a solid foundation for her future role as a chaplain.

2. Master's Degree

A master's degree is typically required for hospice chaplains. The most common advanced degree for chaplains is the Master of Divinity (MDiv), though other relevant degrees such as a Master of Theology (ThM) or Master of Pastoral Counseling (MPC) are also acceptable.

Key Areas of Study:

- Advanced Theology: Deepening understanding of theological concepts and religious practices.

- Pastoral Care: Learning advanced counseling and spiritual care techniques.

- Clinical Pastoral Education (CPE): Gaining practical experience in providing spiritual care in clinical settings.

Example: Master's Program

After completing her bachelor's degree, Jane enrolled in a Master of Divinity program. Her studies included courses on ethics, advanced pastoral counseling, and bereavement care. She also participated in Clinical Pastoral Education, where she gained hands-on experience in a hospital setting.

Clinical Pastoral Education (CPE)

Clinical Pastoral Education is a crucial component of training for hospice chaplains. CPE programs provide practical experience and supervision, helping students develop the skills needed to offer effective spiritual care in clinical environments.

1. CPE Program Structure

CPE programs are typically offered through hospitals, hospices, and theological seminaries. These programs include supervised clinical practice, group discussions, and individual supervision.

Key Components of CPE:

- Clinical Practice: Providing spiritual care to patients and families in real-world settings.

- Supervision: Receiving feedback and guidance from experienced chaplains.

- Group Reflection: Participating in group discussions to reflect on experiences and learn from peers.

Example: CPE Experience

During her CPE program, Jane worked in a hospice facility, providing spiritual care to patients and their families. She participated in regular supervision sessions, where she received feedback on her interactions and discussed ethical dilemmas. This experience was invaluable in developing her skills and confidence as a chaplain.

2. CPE Levels

CPE programs are typically divided into different levels, starting with introductory units and progressing to more advanced training.

Levels of CPE:

- CPE Level I: Introductory training that focuses on developing basic skills in pastoral care and self-awareness.

- CPE Level II: Advanced training that builds on Level I, focusing on specialized skills and deeper self-reflection.

- Supervisory CPE: Training for experienced chaplains who wish to become CPE supervisors, providing guidance and support to CPE students.

Example: Advanced CPE Training

After completing her initial CPE unit, Jane enrolled in a Level II CPE program. This advanced training allowed her to specialize in hospice care, further refining her skills and deepening her understanding of end-of-life issues.

Certification and Professional Development

Certification and ongoing professional development are essential for maintaining high standards of care and staying current with best practices in hospice chaplaincy.

1. Certification

Professional certification demonstrates that a chaplain has met the necessary standards of education, training, and experience. Several organizations offer certification for hospice chaplains.

Certifying Organizations:

- Association of Professional Chaplains (APC): Offers certification for chaplains who meet specific educational and experiential requirements.

- National Association of Catholic Chaplains (NACC): Provides certification for Catholic chaplains.

- National Association of Jewish Chaplains (NAJC): Offers certification for Jewish chaplains.

- Spiritual Care Association (SCA): Provides certification for chaplains from various religious backgrounds.

Certification Requirements:

- Educational Qualifications: A relevant master's degree.

- CPE Units: Completion of required CPE units.

- Clinical Experience: Documented experience in providing spiritual care.

- Ethical Standards: Adherence to professional ethical standards and codes of conduct.

Example: Certification Process

Jane applied for certification through the Association of Professional Chaplains. She submitted documentation of her educational background, CPE units, and clinical experience. After a thorough review, she was awarded certification, recognizing her as a qualified hospice chaplain.

2. Ongoing Professional Development

Continuous learning and professional development are critical for staying current with advancements in hospice care and maintaining the skills necessary for effective chaplaincy.

Professional Development Activities:

- Continuing Education: Participating in workshops, seminars, and online courses.

- Professional Conferences: Attending conferences and networking with other professionals in the field.

- Peer Support Groups: Engaging in peer support groups for mutual learning and encouragement.

- Reading and Research: Keeping up with the latest research and literature in hospice care and spiritual care.

Example: Continuing Education

Jane regularly attended workshops and conferences on hospice care and spiritual counseling. She also participated in a local peer support group for chaplains, where she shared experiences and learned from her colleagues. These activities helped her stay informed about best practices and continue growing as a professional.

Practical Tips for Aspiring Chaplains

1. Seek Mentorship

Finding a mentor who is an experienced chaplain can provide invaluable guidance and support throughout your training and early career.

Example: Jane's Mentor

Jane sought mentorship from an experienced chaplain at her hospice facility. Her mentor provided practical advice, emotional support, and insights into the challenges and rewards of chaplaincy.

Benefits of Mentorship:

- Guidance: Receiving advice on educational and career choices.

- Support: Having a trusted confidant to discuss challenges and successes.

- Networking: Gaining access to professional networks and opportunities.

2. Engage in Self-Reflection

Regular self-reflection helps chaplains understand their motivations, strengths, and areas for growth, ensuring they remain effective and compassionate caregivers.

Example: Jane's Reflection Practices

Jane kept a reflective journal where she documented her experiences, emotions, and learnings. She also engaged in regular meditation and prayer to stay connected to her spiritual practice.

Benefits of Self-Reflection:

- Self-Awareness: Gaining insights into personal strengths and weaknesses.

- Emotional Balance: Managing stress and emotional challenges.

- Professional Growth: Identifying areas for further development and learning.

3. Build a Support Network

Having a strong support network of colleagues, friends, and family is essential for managing the emotional demands of hospice chaplaincy.

Example: Jane's Support Network

Jane maintained close relationships with her fellow chaplains, participated in professional organizations, and stayed connected with her family and friends. This support network provided her with emotional resilience and encouragement.

Benefits of a Support Network:

- Emotional Support: Having trusted individuals to turn to during challenging times.

- Professional Resources: Accessing advice, feedback, and resources from colleagues.

- Personal Balance: Maintaining a healthy work-life balance.

Conclusion: The Path to Becoming a Hospice Chaplain

The path to becoming a hospice chaplain involves rigorous education, practical training, and a commitment to continuous professional development. By following the outlined educational pathways and engaging in ongoing learning, aspiring chaplains can develop the skills and knowledge necessary to provide compassionate and effective spiritual care.

The strategies and examples shared in this chapter highlight the importance of a comprehensive and multidisciplinary approach to training and development. As we continue to explore the role of hospice chaplains in the following chapters, the dedication to education and professional growth stands as a testament to the commitment and resilience required for this sacred vocation.

## CONTINUAL LEARNING

Importance of Ongoing Professional Development and Self-Care

In the field of hospice chaplaincy, continual learning and self-care are essential for maintaining effectiveness, compassion, and resilience. This chapter explores the importance of ongoing professional development and self-care for hospice chaplains, highlighting practical strategies and benefits for both personal and professional growth.

The Need for Ongoing Professional Development

The landscape of hospice care is continually evolving, with new research, best practices, and ethical considerations emerging regularly. For hospice chaplains, staying current with these developments is crucial to providing the highest quality of care to patients and families.

1. Staying Updated with Best Practices

Continual learning ensures that chaplains are informed about the latest best practices in spiritual care, palliative care, and bereavement support.

Example: Chaplain Emily's Professional Development

Chaplain Emily regularly attended workshops and webinars on topics such as advanced grief counseling, cultural competence, and ethical decision-making. This ongoing education helped her stay updated with the latest practices and enhance her skills.

Strategies for Staying Updated:

- Workshops and Seminars: Participate in in-person and online workshops to learn about new developments in hospice care.

- Professional Journals: Subscribe to journals and magazines related to hospice and palliative care.

- Online Courses: Enroll in online courses that offer flexible learning opportunities.

2. Enhancing Skills and Competencies

Continual learning allows chaplains to refine their skills and develop new competencies that enhance their effectiveness in providing spiritual care.

Example: Chaplain James's Skill Enhancement

Chaplain James took a course on trauma-informed care, which equipped him with new techniques for supporting patients and families dealing with traumatic experiences. This additional training made him more adept at addressing complex emotional needs.

Strategies for Enhancing Skills:

- Specialized Training: Pursue specialized training in areas such as trauma-informed care, advanced bereavement support, and cultural competence.

- Certifications: Obtain additional certifications to demonstrate expertise in specific areas of hospice care.

- Peer Learning: Engage in peer learning through study groups and professional networks.

3. Addressing Emerging Ethical Issues

Ongoing professional development helps chaplains navigate emerging ethical issues in hospice care, ensuring they can make informed and compassionate decisions.

Example: Chaplain Maria and Ethical Training

Chaplain Maria attended an ethics seminar that addressed contemporary issues such as end-of-life decision-making and patient autonomy. This training provided her with a deeper understanding of ethical considerations and improved her ability to navigate complex situations.

Strategies for Addressing Ethical Issues:

- Ethics Seminars: Participate in seminars and workshops focused on ethical issues in hospice care.

- Case Studies: Study case studies to understand how ethical dilemmas are resolved in real-world situations.

- Ethics Committees: Join or consult with ethics committees to discuss and address ethical challenges.

The Importance of Self-Care for Chaplains

Self-care is essential for hospice chaplains to manage the emotional demands of their work and maintain their well-being. Practicing self-care ensures that chaplains can provide compassionate care without experiencing burnout or compassion fatigue.

1. Managing Emotional Strain

The work of a hospice chaplain involves constant exposure to grief, loss, and suffering. Effective self-care practices help chaplains manage this emotional strain and maintain their emotional health.

Example: Chaplain David's Self-Care Routine

Chaplain David practiced mindfulness meditation daily, which helped him stay centered and manage stress. He also set aside time for hobbies such as gardening and reading, which provided him with a sense of relaxation and joy.

Strategies for Managing Emotional Strain:

- Mindfulness Practices: Engage in mindfulness practices such as meditation, yoga, or deep breathing exercises.

- Hobbies and Interests: Pursue hobbies and interests that bring relaxation and fulfillment.

- Emotional Boundaries: Set emotional boundaries to prevent becoming overly attached or emotionally overwhelmed.

2. Building a Support Network

Having a strong support network is crucial for chaplains to receive emotional and professional support. This network can include colleagues, mentors, friends, and family.

Example: Chaplain Sarah's Support Network

Chaplain Sarah participated in a peer support group for hospice chaplains, where she shared experiences and received encouragement. She also maintained close relationships with her family and friends, who provided her with emotional support.

Strategies for Building a Support Network:

- Peer Support Groups: Join or form peer support groups with fellow chaplains to share experiences and provide mutual support.

- Mentorship: Seek mentorship from experienced chaplains for guidance and advice.

- Personal Relationships: Maintain strong personal relationships to ensure a well-rounded support system.

3. Regular Self-Reflection

Regular self-reflection helps chaplains understand their motivations, strengths, and areas for growth. This practice is essential for personal and professional development.

Example: Chaplain Emily's Reflection Practices

Chaplain Emily kept a reflective journal where she documented her experiences, emotions, and learnings. She also engaged in regular prayer and spiritual reflection to stay connected to her own faith.

Strategies for Regular Self-Reflection:

- Journaling: Keep a journal to document experiences, thoughts, and emotions.

- Spiritual Practices: Engage in spiritual practices such as prayer, meditation, or contemplation.

- Professional Supervision: Participate in regular supervision sessions to reflect on professional experiences and receive feedback.

Practical Tips for Continual Learning and Self-Care

1. Schedule Time for Professional Development

Set aside dedicated time for ongoing learning and professional development activities.

Example: Chaplain James's Learning Schedule

Chaplain James allocated one afternoon each week for professional development activities, such as attending webinars, reading professional journals, or taking online courses.

Benefits of Scheduled Learning:

- Consistency: Ensures regular engagement with professional development.

- Focus: Provides dedicated time to focus on learning without distractions.

- Progress: Facilitates continuous improvement and skill enhancement.

2. Create a Self-Care Plan

Develop a personalized self-care plan that includes specific activities and practices to maintain emotional and physical well-being.

Example: Chaplain Maria's Self-Care Plan

Chaplain Maria created a self-care plan that included daily mindfulness meditation, weekly exercise sessions, and monthly outings with friends. She also scheduled regular check-ins with her supervisor to discuss emotional challenges.

Components of a Self-Care Plan:

- Daily Practices: Incorporate daily practices such as meditation, exercise, or hobbies.

- Regular Activities: Schedule regular activities that provide relaxation and enjoyment.

- Professional Support: Include regular supervision or counseling sessions for professional support.

3. Engage in Peer Learning and Support

Participate in peer learning and support activities to share experiences, gain new insights, and receive encouragement.

Example: Chaplain Sarah's Peer Group

Chaplain Sarah joined a local peer group for hospice chaplains, where members met monthly to discuss challenges, share resources, and provide mutual support.

Benefits of Peer Learning:

- Shared Experiences: Gain insights from the experiences of others.

- Mutual Support: Provide and receive encouragement and support.

- Collaborative Learning: Learn collaboratively and enhance professional skills.

Case Study: The Impact of Continual Learning and Self-Care

Chaplain: David

Chaplain David recognized the importance of continual learning and self-care in maintaining his effectiveness and well-being as a hospice chaplain. He developed a comprehensive approach to professional development and self-care.

The Chaplain's Approach:

David attended workshops on advanced grief counseling and cultural competence, enhancing his skills and knowledge. He also practiced daily mindfulness meditation and pursued hobbies such as painting and hiking to manage stress. David maintained strong relationships with his peers, participating in regular support group meetings.

The Grace-Filled Moment:

Through continual learning and self-care, David remained compassionate and resilient in his role. His commitment to professional development ensured that he provided the highest quality of care to his patients and families. His self-care practices helped him maintain emotional balance and prevent burnout.

Impact:

David's approach to continual learning and self-care exemplifies the importance of ongoing professional development and personal well-being for hospice chaplains. His dedication to growth and self-care enabled him to provide compassionate and effective spiritual support.

Conclusion: The Commitment to Growth and Well-Being

Continual learning and self-care are essential for hospice chaplains to maintain their effectiveness, compassion, and resilience. By engaging in ongoing professional development and practicing self-care, chaplains can provide high-quality spiritual care while sustaining their own well-being.

The strategies and examples shared in this chapter highlight the importance of a balanced approach to professional growth and personal care. As we continue to explore the role of hospice chaplains in the following chapters, the commitment to continual learning and self-care stands as a testament to the dedication and resilience required for this sacred vocation.

CHAPTER 10

# REFLECTIONS AND FUTURE DIRECTIONS

The Future of Hospice Chaplaincy: Emerging Trends and the Future Landscape of This Field

Hospice chaplaincy is a dynamic and evolving field, continuously adapting to meet the changing needs of patients and their families. As we look to the future, several emerging trends and developments are shaping the landscape of hospice chaplaincy. This chapter explores these trends, reflecting on the current state of the field and anticipating the future directions of hospice chaplaincy.

Emerging Trends in Hospice Chaplaincy

Several key trends are emerging in the field of hospice chaplaincy, driven by advances in technology, shifts in healthcare practices, and evolving societal attitudes toward death and dying.

1. Integration of Technology in Spiritual Care

The use of technology in spiritual care is becoming increasingly prevalent, offering new ways for chaplains to connect with patients and provide support.

Example: Virtual Chaplaincy

Chaplains are utilizing video conferencing tools to provide virtual spiritual care to patients who may be unable to receive in-person visits due to distance, health concerns, or pandemic restrictions. This approach ensures that spiritual support remains accessible to all patients.

Future Implications:

- Accessibility: Technology can enhance accessibility, allowing chaplains to reach patients in remote or underserved areas.

- Continuity of Care: Virtual chaplaincy can provide continuous support even when in-person visits are not possible.

- Innovative Tools: The development of apps and digital resources for spiritual care can offer new ways to support patients and families.

2. Interdisciplinary Collaboration

Interdisciplinary collaboration is becoming a cornerstone of hospice care, with chaplains working closely with healthcare professionals to provide holistic support to patients and families.

Example: Integrated Care Teams

Chaplains are increasingly integrated into multidisciplinary care teams, collaborating with doctors, nurses, social workers, and therapists to address the comprehensive needs of patients.

Future Implications:

- Holistic Care: Enhanced collaboration can ensure that all aspects of a patient's well-being are addressed, including physical, emotional, and spiritual needs.

- Shared Knowledge: Interdisciplinary teams can share knowledge and best practices, improving the quality of care.

- Coordinated Support: Better coordination among team members can lead to more effective and efficient care delivery.

3. Cultural Competence and Inclusivity

As societies become more diverse, the need for culturally competent and inclusive spiritual care is increasingly recognized.

Example: Training Programs

Hospice chaplains are receiving training in cultural competence to better understand and respect the diverse beliefs and practices of their patients.

Future Implications:

- Respectful Care: Improved cultural competence can lead to more respectful and personalized care for patients from diverse backgrounds.

- Inclusive Practices: Chaplains can develop inclusive practices that honor the unique spiritual needs of each patient.

- Diverse Workforce: Encouraging diversity within the chaplaincy workforce can enhance the cultural competence of the field as a whole.

4. Focus on Mental Health and Well-Being

There is a growing recognition of the importance of mental health and well-being in hospice care, with chaplains playing a key role in addressing these aspects.

Example: Mental Health Training

Chaplains are receiving training in mental health support to better address issues such as anxiety, depression, and grief among patients and families.

Future Implications:

- Comprehensive Support: Enhanced mental health training can enable chaplains to provide comprehensive emotional and spiritual support.

- Integrated Care: Integrating mental health support into spiritual care can improve overall patient and family well-being.

- Preventive Measures: Early identification and intervention for mental health issues can prevent complications and improve quality of life.

Reflections on the Current State of Hospice Chaplaincy

The current state of hospice chaplaincy is marked by a commitment to compassionate care, ethical practice, and continuous improvement. Chaplains are dedicated to providing holistic support that addresses the spiritual, emotional, and psychological needs of patients and families.

1. Compassionate Presence

The compassionate presence of chaplains remains a cornerstone of hospice care, providing comfort and support to those at the end of life.

Example: Chaplain Emily's Impact

Chaplain Emily's compassionate presence brought immense comfort to her patients and their families, helping them navigate the challenges of terminal illness with grace and dignity.

2. Ethical Practice

Chaplains adhere to high ethical standards, ensuring that their care is respectful, informed, and centered on the needs and wishes of the patient.

Example: Ethical Dilemmas

Chaplains regularly navigate ethical dilemmas, such as balancing patient autonomy with family desires, maintaining confidentiality, and truth-telling. Their commitment to ethical practice ensures that they provide care that is both compassionate and principled.

3. Continuous Improvement

The field of hospice chaplaincy is characterized by a commitment to continuous improvement, with chaplains engaging in ongoing education and professional development.

Example: Professional Development

Chaplains like James and Maria pursue ongoing training and education to enhance their skills and stay current with best practices in hospice care.

Future Directions for Hospice Chaplaincy

Looking to the future, hospice chaplaincy is poised to continue evolving in response to emerging trends and societal changes. Several key areas of development are anticipated:

1. Enhanced Education and Training

Future chaplains will benefit from enhanced education and training programs that incorporate emerging trends and address the evolving needs of patients and families.

Example: Comprehensive Training Programs

Future training programs may include modules on technology integration, interdisciplinary collaboration, cultural competence, and mental health support, ensuring that chaplains are well-equipped to meet the demands of the field.

2. Increased Research and Evidence-Based Practice

There is a growing emphasis on research and evidence-based practice in hospice chaplaincy, with a focus on measuring the impact of spiritual care and developing best practices.

Example: Research Initiatives

Future research initiatives may explore the effectiveness of virtual chaplaincy, the impact of interdisciplinary collaboration, and the outcomes of culturally competent care.

3. Expanding Access to Spiritual Care

Efforts to expand access to spiritual care will continue, ensuring that all patients and families have the opportunity to receive the support they need.

Example: Outreach Programs

Future outreach programs may focus on underserved communities, rural areas, and marginalized populations, providing spiritual care to those who may have limited access.

4. Integration of Holistic Health Approaches

Holistic health approaches that integrate physical, emotional, and spiritual care will become increasingly important in hospice chaplaincy.

Example: Holistic Care Models

Future models of care may emphasize the integration of complementary therapies, such as art therapy, music therapy, and mindfulness practices, alongside traditional spiritual care.

Conclusion: Embracing the Future of Hospice Chaplaincy

The future of hospice chaplaincy is bright, characterized by innovation, inclusivity, and a deep commitment to compassionate care. As the field continues to evolve, chaplains will play a crucial role in addressing the holistic needs of patients and families, ensuring that they receive the support and comfort they need during the end-of-life journey.

The reflections and future directions shared in this chapter highlight the dynamic nature of hospice chaplaincy and the importance of continual growth and adaptation. As we move forward, the dedication of hospice chaplains to compassionate care, ethical practice, and continuous improvement will remain the foundation of this vital field.

# PERSONAL REFLECTIONS

Final Thoughts from Experienced Chaplains on the Evolution and Future of Their Vocation

As we conclude this exploration of hospice chaplaincy, it is fitting to reflect on the personal insights and experiences of those who have dedicated their lives to this sacred work. The perspectives of experienced chaplains provide valuable lessons on the evolution of the field and offer a glimpse into its future. This chapter shares final thoughts from seasoned chaplains, highlighting their reflections on the past, present, and future of hospice chaplaincy.

Chaplain Emily: The Power of Presence

Reflection:

"My journey as a hospice chaplain has taught me the profound power of presence. In the face of suffering and grief, simply being there for patients and their families can make a world of difference. Over the years, I've seen how a compassionate presence can bring comfort and peace, even in the darkest moments. As our field evolves, I believe this core principle of presence will remain unchanged. Technology and new practices may enhance our work, but the essence of being present, truly present, with those we serve, will always be at the heart of hospice chaplaincy."

Future Vision:

"I envision a future where chaplains are even more integrated into interdisciplinary teams, where our presence is valued not just for the spiritual support we provide, but also for the holistic care we contribute. I see us leveraging technology to reach more people, but never losing sight of the importance of personal connection."

Chaplain James: Embracing Change and Innovation

Reflection:

"The field of hospice chaplaincy has seen significant changes over the years, from advancements in palliative care to a greater understanding of the psychological aspects of dying. I've embraced these changes, learning new techniques and integrating them into my practice. One of the most exciting developments is the use of technology to provide virtual spiritual care. This has opened up new possibilities for reaching patients who might otherwise be isolated. However, it's essential to balance these innovations with the timeless elements of our work — empathy, compassion, and deep listening."

Future Vision:

"I believe the future of hospice chaplaincy will be marked by continuous innovation. We will need to stay adaptable, incorporating new methods and tools while remaining grounded in our core values. I look forward to seeing more research that highlights the impact of our work, helping to solidify the role of chaplains in holistic healthcare."

Chaplain Maria: The Importance of Cultural Competence

Reflection:

"Throughout my career, I've encountered patients from diverse cultural and religious backgrounds. Each experience has underscored the importance of cultural competence in providing effective spiritual care. Understanding and respecting different traditions and beliefs have been key to connecting with patients and their families on a deeper level. As society becomes more diverse, I see cultural competence as an area that will continue to grow in importance for chaplains."

Future Vision:

"I hope to see more training programs focused on cultural competence and inclusivity. Future chaplains will need to be well-versed in a variety of cultural practices and religious traditions to serve our increasingly diverse patient population effectively. Embracing this diversity will enrich our practice and enhance the care we provide."

Chaplain David: The Role of Self-Care and Resilience
Reflection:

"One of the most important lessons I've learned is the necessity of self-care. The emotional demands of hospice chaplaincy can be intense, and without proper self-care, it's easy to become overwhelmed. I've found that maintaining a balance between work and personal life, engaging in regular supervision, and practicing mindfulness have been crucial for my well-being. As we move forward, I believe that fostering resilience among chaplains will be essential for sustaining our capacity to care for others."

Future Vision:

"I envision a future where chaplains are supported by robust self-care programs and peer support networks. By prioritizing our own well-being, we can continue to provide high-quality care to our patients. Resilience training and mental health resources will be integral parts of chaplaincy education and ongoing professional development."

Chaplain Sarah: The Evolving Role of Chaplains
Reflection:

"The role of hospice chaplains has evolved significantly during my career. We've gone from being seen primarily as religious figures to being recognized as integral members of the healthcare team, providing holistic care that addresses the spiritual, emotional, and psychological needs of patients. This evolution has been incredibly rewarding, as it highlights the value of our work and the impact we have on patient care. I've also witnessed the increasing importance of interfaith dialogue and collaboration, which has enriched my practice and broadened my understanding of spirituality."

Future Vision:

"In the future, I see chaplains playing an even more prominent role in healthcare. We will be advocates for holistic care, working alongside medical professionals to ensure that all aspects of a patient's well-being are addressed. I also foresee greater emphasis on interfaith and multicultural approaches, ensuring that chaplaincy services are inclusive and accessible to all."

Conclusion: A Bright Future for Hospice Chaplaincy

The personal reflections of experienced chaplains underscore the profound impact of their work and the evolving nature of the field. As hospice chaplaincy continues to grow and adapt, the dedication to compassionate presence, cultural competence, innovation, self-care, and holistic care will remain central to its mission.

The future of hospice chaplaincy is bright, marked by a commitment to continual learning, ethical practice, and the integration of new technologies and methodologies. By embracing these changes while staying true to the core values of empathy, compassion, and deep listening, hospice chaplains will continue to provide invaluable support to patients and families during the end-of-life journey.

As we look ahead, the reflections and insights of seasoned chaplains serve as a guiding light, illuminating the path forward and inspiring future generations of chaplains to carry on this vital and sacred work. The evolution of hospice chaplaincy will undoubtedly bring new challenges and opportunities, but with a steadfast commitment to holistic and compassionate care, the future is filled with promise and hope.

CONCLUSION

---

## **SUMMARIZING KEY POINTS**

Recap of the Key Insights and Lessons from the Book

This book has journeyed through the multifaceted and deeply rewarding field of hospice chaplaincy, exploring its various dimensions, challenges, and future directions. The following key insights and lessons encapsulate the essence of what has been covered:

1. The Role of a Hospice Chaplain:

- Hospice chaplains provide spiritual, emotional, and psychological support to patients and their families during the end-of-life journey. They are integral members of the healthcare team, addressing holistic needs through compassionate presence and deep listening.

2. Ethical Dilemmas and Professional Boundaries:

- Chaplains navigate complex ethical dilemmas, balancing patient autonomy, family desires, and medical recommendations. Maintaining professional boundaries ensures effective and ethical care, preventing emotional burnout and over-involvement.

3. Training and Development:

- A comprehensive education in theology, pastoral care, and clinical pastoral education (CPE) forms the foundation for aspiring chaplains. Ongoing professional development and self-care are crucial for sustaining compassion and resilience in this demanding field.

4. Inclusive and Culturally Competent Care:

- Providing culturally competent and inclusive spiritual care is essential in a diverse society. Chaplains must understand and respect the varied religious and cultural backgrounds of patients, fostering an environment of inclusivity and personalized care.

5. Continual Learning and Self-Care:

- Continual learning ensures that chaplains stay updated with best practices and emerging trends in hospice care. Self-care practices, including mindfulness, peer support, and balanced work-life integration, are vital for managing emotional strain and maintaining well-being.

6. The Future of Hospice Chaplaincy:

- The field is evolving with the integration of technology, interdisciplinary collaboration, and a focus on mental health and well-being. Future trends include enhanced training programs, increased research, and expanded access to spiritual care.

7. Personal Reflections and Future Directions:

- Experienced chaplains emphasize the power of presence, the importance of cultural competence, and the need for continual adaptation and resilience. Their insights provide valuable guidance for the future of hospice chaplaincy.

Encouragement and Inspiration: Words of Encouragement for Current and Aspiring Hospice Chaplains

To all current and aspiring hospice chaplains, your dedication to this sacred vocation is both inspiring and vital. The journey of a hospice chaplain is filled with profound moments of connection, compassion, and grace. Here are some words of encouragement as you continue or begin this meaningful path:

Embrace the Power of Presence:

Your presence alone can bring immense comfort and peace to those at the end of life. Remember that being there, truly present, with your patients and their families is a powerful act of compassion.

Continually Learn and Grow:

The field of hospice chaplaincy is ever-evolving. Embrace opportunities for professional development and continual learning. Stay curious, seek new knowledge, and be open to adapting your practices to meet the changing needs of those you serve.

Prioritize Self-Care:

Your well-being is essential to providing effective care. Make self-care a priority, engage in practices that nourish your mind, body, and spirit, and seek support from peers and mentors. By taking care of yourself, you ensure that you can sustainably care for others.

Foster Inclusivity and Cultural Competence:

The diverse backgrounds of your patients and their families are a rich tapestry that enhances the caregiving experience. Strive to understand and respect their unique beliefs and practices, creating an inclusive environment where all feel valued and supported.

Stay Resilient and Hopeful:

The work of a hospice chaplain can be emotionally challenging, but it is also incredibly rewarding. Hold on to the moments of connection and grace that remind you of the profound impact of your work. Stay resilient, and find hope in the knowledge that you are providing invaluable support during one of life's most significant transitions.

Look to the Future with Optimism:

The future of hospice chaplaincy is filled with promise. Embrace new technologies, interdisciplinary approaches, and innovative practices that enhance your ability to provide holistic care. Your role will continue to evolve, and your commitment to compassionate, ethical care will remain at the heart of this field.

Final Thoughts:

You are a beacon of light in the lives of those facing the end of life. Your work brings comfort, peace, and dignity to patients and their families. As you continue on this path, know that your efforts are deeply appreciated and profoundly impactful.

May you find strength in your calling, joy in your connections, and peace in your heart as you journey forward in the sacred vocation of hospice chaplaincy. Your dedication and compassion make a world of difference, and the future is brighter because of you.

# APPENDIX

---

## RESOURCES FOR CHAPLAINS

Books

1. "The Art of Dying: Living Fully into the Life to Come" by Rob Moll

   - Explores the spiritual and practical aspects of end-of-life care from a Christian perspective.

2. "Being with Dying: Cultivating Compassion and Fearlessness in the Presence of Death" by Joan Halifax

   - Provides insights and practices for accompanying those at the end of life with compassion and mindfulness.

3. "Final Gifts: Understanding the Special Awareness, Needs, and Communications of the Dying" by Maggie Callanan and Patricia Kelley

   - Offers guidance on recognizing and responding to the unique needs of dying patients.

4. "The Four Things That Matter Most: A Book About Living" by Ira Byock

- Focuses on the essential communications and emotional tasks that can bring peace and healing at the end of life.

5. "Dying Well: Peace and Possibilities at the End of Life" by Ira Byock

- Discusses how to achieve a meaningful and peaceful end-of-life experience.

6. "Spiritual Care at the End of Life: The Chaplain as a 'Hopeful Presence'" by Steve Nolan

- Examines the role of chaplains in providing spiritual care and hope to terminally ill patients.

7. "The Soul of Care: The Moral Education of a Husband and a Doctor" by Arthur Kleinman

- Explores the deep connection between caregiving and the moral and spiritual dimensions of life.

8. "Hospice and Palliative Care: The Essential Guide" by Stephen R. Connor

- A comprehensive resource on hospice and palliative care practices, including spiritual care.

9. "Caring for the Dying: The Doula Approach to a Meaningful Death" by Henry Fersko-Weiss

- Introduces the concept of end-of-life doulas and their role in providing compassionate care.

10. "Sacred Dying: Creating Rituals for Embracing the End of Life" by Megory Anderson

- Offers practical advice on creating rituals to honor the end-of-life journey.

Organizations

1. Association of Professional Chaplains (APC)

- Website: [www.professionalchaplains.org](http://www.professionalchaplains.org)

- Provides certification, education, and support for professional chaplains.

2. National Association of Catholic Chaplains (NACC)

- Website: [www.nacc.org](http://www.nacc.org)

- Offers certification and resources for Catholic chaplains.

3. National Association of Jewish Chaplains (NAJC)

- Website: [www.najc.org](http://www.najc.org)

- Provides certification and support for Jewish chaplains.

4. Spiritual Care Association (SCA)

-                                                                Website:
[www.spiritualcareassociation.org](http://www.spiritualcarea
ssociation.org)

- Offers certification, education, and resources for chaplains from various religious backgrounds.

5. Hospice Foundation of America (HFA)

-                                                                Website:
[www.hospicefoundation.org](http://www.hospicefoundatio
n.org)

- Provides resources and education on hospice care, including spiritual care.

6. Center to Advance Palliative Care (CAPC)

- Website: [www.capc.org](http://www.capc.org)

- Offers training and resources for palliative care professionals.

7. The Hastings Center

-                                                                Website:
[www.thehastingscenter.org](http://www.thehastingscenter.
org)

- Focuses on ethical issues in healthcare, including end-of-life care.

8. International End of Life Doula Association (INELDA)

-                                                          Website: [www.inelda.org](http://www.inelda.org)

- Provides training and certification for end-of-life doulas.

9. American Academy of Hospice and Palliative Medicine (AAHPM)

-                                                          Website: [www.aahpm.org](http://www.aahpm.org)

- Professional organization for hospice and palliative care physicians, offering resources for interdisciplinary team members.

10. National Hospice and Palliative Care Organization (NHPCO)

-                                                          Website: [www.nhpco.org](http://www.nhpco.org)

- Offers resources, education, and advocacy for hospice and palliative care providers.

Training Programs

1. Clinical Pastoral Education (CPE) Programs

- Offered by hospitals, hospices, and theological seminaries.

- Provides practical training and supervision in pastoral care.

2. Hospice and Palliative Care Training Programs

- Many universities and medical centers offer specialized training in hospice and palliative care, including spiritual care components.

3. Certification Programs for Chaplains

- Association of Professional Chaplains (APC)

- Certification for professional chaplains.

- National Association of Catholic Chaplains (NACC)

- Certification for Catholic chaplains.

- National Association of Jewish Chaplains (NAJC)

- Certification for Jewish chaplains.

- Spiritual Care Association (SCA)

- Certification for chaplains from various religious backgrounds.

4. Workshops and Continuing Education

- Many professional organizations, such as the APC, NACC, NAJC, and SCA, offer workshops, webinars, and continuing education courses on various aspects of hospice chaplaincy.

5. Graduate Programs in Theology, Pastoral Care, and Counseling

- Master of Divinity (MDiv), Master of Theology (ThM), and Master of Pastoral Counseling (MPC) programs offered by seminaries and universities.

6. End-of-Life Doula Training

- International End of Life Doula Association (INELDA)

- Provides training and certification for end-of-life doulas, focusing on compassionate care and support.

7. Palliative Care Education

- Center to Advance Palliative Care (CAPC)

- Offers training and resources for palliative care professionals, including spiritual care education.

These resources, including books, organizations, and training programs, provide valuable support and education for current and aspiring hospice chaplains. By engaging with these resources, chaplains can continue to grow in their vocation, enhance their skills, and provide compassionate, holistic care to those at the end of life.

---

## PERSONAL REFLECTION AND GROUP DISCUSSION

Personal Reflection Questions

1. What inspired you to pursue a vocation in hospice chaplaincy?

- Reflect on your initial motivations and how they align with your current experiences.

2. How do you define the role of a hospice chaplain in the context of holistic care?

- Consider the various dimensions of care you provide and how they contribute to the overall well-being of patients and families.

3. What are some of the most profound moments you have experienced as a hospice chaplain?

- Reflect on specific instances that have deeply impacted you and shaped your approach to spiritual care.

4. How do you maintain professional boundaries while providing compassionate care?

- Think about strategies you use to balance empathy and professional detachment.

5. What challenges have you faced in your role, and how have you overcome them?

- Identify specific challenges and the methods you have employed to address them.

6. How do you practice self-care to manage the emotional demands of hospice chaplaincy?

- Reflect on your self-care routines and their effectiveness in maintaining your well-being.

7. In what ways have you seen the field of hospice chaplaincy evolve during your career?

- Consider changes in practices, attitudes, and integration with other healthcare disciplines.

8. How do you incorporate cultural competence and inclusivity into your spiritual care practices?

- Think about your approach to understanding and respecting diverse beliefs and practices.

9. What are your hopes for the future of hospice chaplaincy?

- Reflect on how you envision the field evolving and the impact it can have on patients and families.

10. How do you stay motivated and inspired in your work as a hospice chaplain?

- Identify sources of inspiration and motivation that sustain you in your vocation.

Group Discussion Questions

1. How do we, as a team of chaplains, ensure that we provide holistic care that addresses the physical, emotional, and spiritual needs of our patients?

- Discuss strategies for interdisciplinary collaboration and comprehensive care.

2. What are some ethical dilemmas we have encountered in our work, and how did we resolve them?

- Share experiences and insights on navigating ethical challenges.

3. In what ways can we improve our cultural competence to better serve our diverse patient population?

- Explore opportunities for training, education, and community engagement.

4. How can we support each other in maintaining professional boundaries and managing emotional strain?

- Discuss the importance of peer support and strategies for mutual encouragement.

5. What innovations or technologies have we integrated into our practice, and how have they impacted our care?

- Reflect on the role of technology and new practices in enhancing spiritual care.

6. How do we ensure that our continuing education and professional development align with the evolving needs of our patients?

- Consider ways to prioritize ongoing learning and skills enhancement.

7. What are some best practices we have developed for providing virtual spiritual care, and what challenges remain?

- Share experiences and solutions related to virtual chaplaincy.

8. How can we better advocate for the role of chaplains within the broader healthcare team?

- Discuss strategies for highlighting the importance and impact of spiritual care.

9. In what ways can we involve patients' families more effectively in the care process?

- Explore methods for enhancing family engagement and support.

10. What are our collective goals for the future of our hospice chaplaincy program, and how can we work together to achieve them?

- Set shared objectives and discuss actionable steps for future growth and improvement.

These reflection questions are designed to encourage personal introspection and foster meaningful group discussions among hospice chaplains. By engaging with these questions, chaplains can deepen their understanding of their vocation, share valuable insights, and collaboratively enhance their practice of providing compassionate, holistic care to patients and families at the end of life.

# REFERENCES

---

## CITED WORKS


1. Byock, Ira. Dying Well: Peace and Possibilities at the End of Life. Riverhead Books, 1997.

- A foundational text on achieving a meaningful and peaceful end-of-life experience.

2. Byock, Ira. The Four Things That Matter Most: A Book About Living. Atria Books, 2004.

- Explores essential communications and emotional tasks that can bring peace and healing at the end of life.

3. Callanan, Maggie, and Patricia Kelley. Final Gifts: Understanding the Special Awareness, Needs, and Communications of the Dying. Bantam Books, 1992.

- Provides guidance on recognizing and responding to the unique needs of dying patients.

4. Connor, Stephen R. Hospice and Palliative Care: The Essential Guide. Routledge, 2009.

- A comprehensive resource on hospice and palliative care practices, including spiritual care.

5. Fersko-Weiss, Henry. Caring for the Dying: The Doula Approach to a Meaningful Death. Conari Press, 2017.

- Introduces the concept of end-of-life doulas and their role in providing compassionate care.

6. Halifax, Joan. Being with Dying: Cultivating Compassion and Fearlessness in the Presence of Death. Shambhala Publications, 2008.

- Provides insights and practices for accompanying those at the end of life with compassion and mindfulness.

7. Kleinman, Arthur. The Soul of Care: The Moral Education of a Husband and a Doctor. Viking, 2019.

- Explores the deep connection between caregiving and the moral and spiritual dimensions of life.

8. Moll, Rob. The Art of Dying: Living Fully into the Life to Come. IVP Books, 2010.

- Explores the spiritual and practical aspects of end-of-life care from a Christian perspective.

9. Nolan, Steve. Spiritual Care at the End of Life: The Chaplain as a 'Hopeful Presence'. Jessica Kingsley Publishers, 2012.

- Examines the role of chaplains in providing spiritual care and hope to terminally ill patients.

10. Anderson, Megory. Sacred Dying: Creating Rituals for Embracing the End of Life. Da Capo Press, 2003.

- Offers practical advice on creating rituals to honor the end-of-life journey.

Online Resources

1. Association of Professional Chaplains (APC). Website: [www.professionalchaplains.org](http://www.professionalchaplains.org)

- Provides certification, education, and support for professional chaplains.

2. National Association of Catholic Chaplains (NACC). Website: [www.nacc.org](http://www.nacc.org)

- Offers certification and resources for Catholic chaplains.

3. National Association of Jewish Chaplains (NAJC). Website: [www.najc.org](http://www.najc.org)

- Provides certification and support for Jewish chaplains.

4. Spiritual Care Association (SCA). Website: [www.spiritualcareassociation.org](http://www.spiritualcareassociation.org)

- Offers certification, education, and resources for chaplains from various religious backgrounds.

5. Hospice Foundation of America (HFA). Website: [www.hospicefoundation.org](http://www.hospicefoundation.org)

- Provides resources and education on hospice care, including spiritual care.

6. Center to Advance Palliative Care (CAPC). Website: [www.capc.org](http://www.capc.org)

- Offers training and resources for palliative care professionals.

7. The Hastings Center. Website: [www.thehastingscenter.org](http://www.thehastingscenter.org)

- Focuses on ethical issues in healthcare, including end-of-life care.

8. International End of Life Doula Association (INELDA). Website: [www.inelda.org](http://www.inelda.org)

- Provides training and certification for end-of-life doulas.

9. American Academy of Hospice and Palliative Medicine (AAHPM). Website: [www.aahpm.org](http://www.aahpm.org)

- Professional organization for hospice and palliative care physicians, offering resources for interdisciplinary team members.

10. National Hospice and Palliative Care Organization (NHPCO).                                Website: [www.nhpco.org](http://www.nhpco.org)

- Offers resources, education, and advocacy for hospice and palliative care providers.

These references provide a comprehensive overview of the foundational texts, organizations, and online resources that support the practice and development of hospice chaplaincy. By engaging with these materials, chaplains can enhance their knowledge, skills, and ability to provide compassionate, holistic care to those at the end of life.